Melissa Kim Corter's

Apothecary for the Afflicted

Shadow Work for Invisible Wounds

Published by Muse Oracle Press Pty Ltd 2025

Apothecary for the Afflicted – Shadow Work for Invisible Wounds

ISBN: 978-1-76358-695-6

Cover design by Muse Oracle Press

Published by Muse Oracle Press Pty Ltd, 2025

www.museoraclepress.com

Distributed by Red Wheel Weiser

www.redwheelweiser.com

This book is a work of personal insight and reflection. It is not intended as a substitute for professional medical, psychological, or psychiatric advice, diagnosis, or treatment. Always seek the advice of a qualified health provider with any questions you may have regarding a medical or mental health condition.

"Knowing your own darkness is
the best method for dealing with
the darknesses of other people."

—C.G. Jung

Dedication

To the terrible Baba Yagas I've endured on the path. I am grateful for the countless ways you attempted to kill my spirit, separate me from my instincts, and rob me of my power. Your poison stopped working. The greatest revenge has been the rescue of my soul, the realization that you never had the power... but now, we both know it.

Foreword to *Apothecary for the Afflicted:*
Shadow Work for Invisible Wounds

by Cyndi Brannen, PhD
Author of Entering Hekate's Garden: The Magick, Medicine and Mystery of
Plant Spirit Witchcraft, Entering Hekate's Cave: The Journey Through Darkness
to Wholeness, and Keeping Her Keys: An Introduction to Hekate's Modern
Witchcraft
https://keepingherkeys.com/

Apothecary for the Afflicted: Shadow Work for Invisible Wounds by Melissa
Kim Corter explores the theme of shadow work, urging readers to confront their
inner struggles for personal growth and healing. Through personal anecdotes and
folk tales, supported by wonderful prompts for personal inquiry, she emphasizes
the importance of individual narratives in the healing process. The book serves as a
supportive guide for self-discovery, addressing trauma and societal pressures while
advocating for the acknowledgment of one's shadows. By embracing both light and
dark aspects, readers are encouraged to reconnect with their true selves, leading to
empowerment and a more authentic life.

One of the biggest choices we have is whether or not to face our own shadow, to
go into our own messiness, to see what gold can be found underneath the piles of
pain and despair. Melissa Kim Corter goes bravely into those messy piles that lurk in
our shadows. Throughout *Apothecary for the Afflicted: Shadow Work for Invisible
Wounds*, she guides the reader into their own darkness, with a firm foundation of
depth psychology, to weave a web of support around all those brave enough to shine
the light on the parts of ourselves that aren't ready for social media.

There is a phrase from alchemy that speaks to the treasure found in excavating our
shadows. *"Aurum nostrum non est aurum vulgi,"* from the *Rosarium Philosophorum*,
affirms that the quest for wholeness requires mining of the soul to transform the unrefined
into our unique wealth—that of the soul. Indeed, "our gold is not ordinary" speaks to the
very personal nature of transforming our past wounds into sources of power.

There is gold in our shadow. There is beauty and illumination in the mess when we
intentionally go into our personal darkness. One of my favorite things about this book
is the way she advocates for personal narratives as our individual treasuries. In all of my
teaching and in my books, particularly *Entering Hekate's Cave*, which is dedicated to
healing the shadow, what I have discovered is that we write our way to gold.

Melissa's prompts, her reflections, and the stories she shares are all amazing keys that can unlock the richness contained in our own shadows. Go gently yet boldly into this work. Go with resolve. Know that you are stronger than you think and that the forthcoming pages are designed with you in mind. Melissa has done this work herself, on herself. I have been teaching, writing, and working with individuals for decades to help them find that wholeness that can only be found through that journey of darkness, where we emerge whole unto ourselves, more authentic, more empowered, and enlightened. This book will help you mine your personal gold.

Like the phases of the moon, we need the waning times. We need to intentionally approach that dark moon. And within that dark moon, through the words of the book and our writings that the book will undoubtedly inspire, we'll find the golden magic of that most sacred time, when the moon hides her face, creating a velvet darkness, a safe womb for exploring our own inner mysteries. Melissa is a teacher and companion with us on the journey.

She understands that family dynamics, previous trauma, feelings of invalidation, and generally living in a world that overemphasizes toxic positivity, spiritual bypassing, and way too much love and light, lead us away from our personal gold mine. She knows that superficial quick fixes ultimately are fools' gold. Without deep lunar work in the shadow realm, we are without the tools required to transmute pain into personal liberation. The moon needs the sun, and the sun needs the moon. We need our own darkness. We need our own shadows.

And the journey is not to kill the shadow, but to understand the shadow. The gold is found by holding the shadow's hand and saying, "What do you have to teach me?" Melissa offers to hold our other hand and lead us through this incredible journey of shadow healing. While I was reading this book, a second alchemical phrase kept circumambulating around in my head: *"Eadem mutata resurgo,"* which translates to "Although changed, I arise the same." This is what this book has the potential to do. We are not fundamentally broken. We are whole, divine creatures. But what can happen is that the shadow overrides the soul. There is no harmony or equanimity in the two. When this happens, we become disconnected from our soul, from our authenticity, and from our true calling in this life. Melissa can guide us gently, with clarity and purpose, back to that place of harmony where shadow and soul coexist, like *The Lovers* card in Tarot.

May you journey well with this book.
Yours in the Shadows,
Cyndi Brannen, PhD

Foreword to *Apothecary for the Afflicted: Shadow Work for Invisible Wounds*

By Stacey Shelby, PhD
www.drstaceyshelby.com
Author of *Tracking the Wild Woman Archetype* (2018) and
Love and Soul-Making (2022)

There is an undeniable call in the human psyche to return to its most authentic state, a yearning to retrieve what has been lost, denied, or cast aside. This call, though often unheard amidst the noise of modern existence, is the whisper of the soul, the deepest and most instinctual aspect of the psyche that has been socialized out of us. In *Apothecary for the Afflicted*, Melissa Kim Corter invites the reader into the realm of shadow, a landscape both feared and revered, where the forgotten aspects of the self wait to be unearthed and reclaimed. It offers the reader who is willing to embark on this journey a powerful elixir for healing, weaving specific fairytales as remedies tailored to different types of emotional and psychological wounds. This is no ordinary book; it is a guide to navigating the unseen wounds that shape our inner world and, ultimately, our external lives.

In my work, I have spent years tracking the wild woman archetype—the part of us that is closest to nature, to instinct, to unbridled creativity and truth. What I have found is that shadow work is essential in this pursuit. The shadow, as understood in the field of depth psychology, is not simply the repository for our fears, wounds, and repressed emotions. It is also the dwelling place of our greatest gifts, our alchemical gold, our intuition, our capacity for deep embodiment, and the knowledge of our own psyche. To work with the shadow is to work with projection, a psychological mechanism by which we attribute disowned parts of ourselves onto others. This book masterfully illuminates how projection is both a trap and a key: it entangles us in unconscious narratives but also provides a pathway to reclaiming what has been lost.

Corter offers the reader an opportunity to explore shadow work not as an act of self-punishment, but as an act of integration. When we embrace what we have been conditioned to reject, we not only reclaim our wholeness but also our soma, the wisdom of the body. It is through reconnecting with the body that we learn to listen to our instincts, to hear the subtle voice of the psyche, and to trust in our own deep knowing. This is the alchemy of shadow work—transforming what was once considered dark and undesirable into strength, wisdom, and self-possession. True transformation is found in the willingness to embrace discomfort, to sit in the unknown, and to listen to what emerges from the depths of the psyche. The wild woman (or wild man) does not fear the dark; they know it as the fertile ground from which deep wisdom is born.

The book also invites us to engage with symbolism, fairy tales, and our macabre fascinations, understanding that these cultural and personal myths hold the keys to our deeper knowing. Why do certain stories captivate us? What is the meaning behind our attractions and repulsions? In engaging these symbols with curiosity rather than fear, we unravel the hidden messages of our own psyche. These symbols, often dismissed as mere fiction or frivolity, are in fact encoded maps leading us to self-revelation. The tales of the old crone, the devouring mother, the trickster, and the hidden child all carry wisdom for those who are willing to seek it. When we work with these symbols, we allow the unconscious to reveal its deeper truths, offering a bridge between the known and unknown aspects of ourselves.

Apothecary for the Afflicted is structured to guide the reader through an intimate journey of self-discovery. Each chapter combines analysis, fairytales, journal prompts, and deep introspection to create an accessible yet profound framework for engaging with one's personal shadow. By working through the provided exercises, the reader is invited to explore and integrate aspects of the self that have been hidden, repressed, or misunderstood. This multi-faceted approach makes shadow work both tangible and transformative, offering a practical methodology for deep psychological inquiry. The inclusion of reflective journaling ensures that the reader moves beyond intellectual understanding into embodied wisdom, engaging the shadow not as an abstract concept but as a lived experience.

The process of shadow integration is not merely about uncovering past wounds but about recognizing the potency of what has been buried. Within the shadow reside not only the aspects of ourselves we have been taught to fear, but also our greatest strengths. The voice that was silenced in childhood, the intuitive knowing that was dismissed, the creative energy that was forced into conformity—these are all waiting to be reclaimed. True shadow work is not about simply healing past wounds but about re-membering (after dismemberment) the wholeness that has always been ours. This book provides a means for doing just that, guiding the reader through exercises that invite them to name and reclaim their hidden gifts.

What I most appreciate about this book is its recognition that shadow work is not merely about self-exploration; it is also about transformation at the collective level. The world is riddled with projection, with blame, with hostility and division. We externalize our discontent onto others rather than recognizing it as part of our own psychic terrain. But to own our shadow is to own our impact in the world. As we become more ourselves, we become more unified—not just within, but in the world at large. This is the tending of the *anima mundi*, the world's soul. Shadow work is not only an inward journey, but a radical act of healing the collective unconscious.

Engaging in this work is an act of reclamation, one that shifts the narrative away from separation and toward unity. As we reclaim our projections, we become less entangled in the endless cycle of blame and more capable of meaningful action. Rather than feeding division, we cultivate the ability to hold complexity—to see the world not in stark binaries of good and evil, but in the richness of its nuance. This shift allows us to engage with the world in a more conscious and compassionate way, offering healing not just to ourselves, but to the communities and relationships we inhabit.

To engage with this book is to engage with the hidden realms of the self, to venture into the dark in search of the philosopher's stone—the inner transformation that leads to outer change. It is a call to courage, a call to wholeness, and ultimately, a call to live with greater depth, authenticity, and responsibility. This book is an invitation to go beyond simplistic narratives of good and bad, light and dark, and to embrace the full complexity of who we are. Only then can we hope to tend to ourselves, each other, and the world with wisdom, compassion, and true presence. May those who embark on this journey do so with a spirit of curiosity and a willingness to meet themselves fully, for it is in that meeting that true healing begins.

Table of Contents

Introduction: She Who Reads This Book 13

How to use Apothecary for the Afflicted 17

Chapter 01. Initiated
She Who Is Thrown into Darkness 29

Chapter 02. Inherited
She Who Holds Darkness 51

Chapter 03. Haunted
She Who Knows Secrets 77

Chapter 04. Dismembered
She Who Is in Pieces. 101

Chapter 05. Poisoned
She Who Consumes Darkness 123

Chapter 06. Numb
She Who Is Frozen 147

Chapter 07. Decomposed
She Who Breaks Down 169

Chapter 08. Deceived
She Who Is Hunted 193

Acknowledgments 220

About the Author 221

Introduction: She Who Reads This Book

*I*f you hold this book in your hands, it's likely you feel deeply. Either a highly sensitive person or empath, you have an uncanny sense of knowing, yet sometimes struggle to understand the patterns that plague you. You have a depth that can be unsettling for others, leaving you feeling frequently misunderstood. You do your best to create those boundaries, and still, you continue to abandon or betray yourself on some level.

Drawn to the darker side of people, circumstances, and events, you see through illusions and spot deception a mile away. You have gathered the pieces of yourself, collecting and salvaging the countless fragments of the past, so you can make sense of impactful, sometimes tragic, moments. These events have changed you on some level. As powerful as you are, as intuitive and aware, you sense it's not enough and never has been. There is more to discover; you know this and have tried countless ways to unlock the mysterious and forbidden rooms within the psyche.

Sure, you have healed from difficult and terrible things, yet somewhere in soma (body) and psyche (soul), and in those pieces you scramble to collect, a few stories remain. There is a longing to channel the wisdom and speak the truth, yet an unconscious fear lingers when it comes to embracing your darkness, your depth.

You've probably heard of the shadow, but still, you find yourself caught in an emotional web. Suspended in the web, you know something deeper is at work within you, orchestrating and enabling this malicious cycle. You have been unconsciously taught to avoid discomfort, to only speak of your desires as if they are already here. To be mindful of your thoughts and how they shape your reality, yet all this effort has left you tired and trapped in a repetitive cycle. You are wise yet blind to the origin of some of your troubles. Maybe you're fed up with being told to meditate and focus on the positive, yearning to unleash the rage in your belly and rekindle the fire of your soul.

If only something could help reveal your power and teach you how to express anger and rage. If only you could permit yourself to pour out the terrible things you pretend not to feel. If only there were a way to fall in love with your darkness.

Sick of being the good girl, nauseated over spiritual language coated in flowery poetics, all the things that keep you further from the feral force that begs for a place to be held, seen, and honored. Maybe you've dabbled in micro-dosing, breathwork, astrology, and human design with bookshelves lined with musings on tarot, prosperity, and rebirthing. You may be acclimated with your inner child, yet you feel in your soul there is so much more.

Maybe you long to be the woman who runs with the wolves and not just read about her.

You have lots to say, yet you don't always have the words to capture the stirring in your bones. You want to know what to do, how to go about it, and be guided, yet have permission to be unhinged. You want to be called out but in a safe way.

Are you tired of hiding and feeling invisible? Do you love the idea of rituals yet feel out of touch with your magic? Maybe you binge podcasts about rewilding and connecting with your soul; you love candles and wild, witchy things. Does a part of you have an affinity for dark matters, such as true crime or psychological thrillers? Perhaps you don't fear your light but fear your depths and are ready to explore them safely and creatively.

You are in the right place.

I was fed up with lame prompts that lacked depth, rolling my eyes every time a coach, yoga teacher, or generic healer invited me to "welcome all parts of who I am." In my 20-plus years of facilitating shadow work, I've learned a simple truth: when a prompt skims the surface, the answer will lack depth. I know how to go deep, bring people into the underbelly of what troubles them, and explore what keeps them stuck and emotionally divided. We must be willing to play with a healthy level of intensity to bring things to the surface, or the skeletons in the closet will continue to haunt us.

It took a long time before I began to truly value the dark side of the human psyche, let alone my own repulsive, guilty, shameful qualities. Honoring the unruly and unholy qualities allows other parts of my authentic self to thrive. The opportunities become richer and more genuine, mirroring this dynamic in intriguing ways. As we seek out shadow, it isn't just to honor the darkness; it's to express the light in a more genuine form that aligns with the unfolding of our individual and unique souls. This is how we mend invisible psychic wounds.

How to use Apothecary for the Afflicted

Unique stories, healing metaphors, and hidden processes are embedded throughout this book. Each chapter combines captivating imagery to enhance the transformative potential within the stories and fairy tales. You will find evocative ideas infused with psychological knowledge and snippets to explain the psychodynamics of the human shadow.

This book is intentionally designed to reveal your blind spots, activate emotion, and guide you to confront the tricky elements stirring within.

There may be times when you recoil while reading a certain idea or theme; something might even prompt you to step back, put the book away, or pass it along to someone else. Try to stay with this inner tension. This is evidence of an alchemical process underway. Resistance is not a signal to give up; it is a doorway into something unexplored, something deeper. There are journal prompts throughout—do them and take them seriously.

Shadow work includes facing the parts of us that continue to splurge on products, books, and programs without doing the work. You must do the work; there are vital practices here for you. The paradox here is only *you* know what doing the work means for you. There are moments when stepping away lets ideas take root and percolate within the cauldron of the psyche; other times it may denote avoidance or denial. Shadow work can breathe new life into dead matters while resurrecting the soul of a long-forgotten dream. Some have found purpose in tragedy, meaning in the messiest of situations and circumstances. This book is a tool; it was created to bring psychic debris to the surface, to reveal sneaky, stubborn, and insidious patterns.

The shadow will reveal itself as you tune in and dive into the menagerie of potent tales, enticing imagery, and intentional prompts. As you continue journaling and moving through the material, the ego, a critical part of our psyche (I refer to it as the gatekeeper), will soften its resistance and help you see through illusions in your innermost thoughts and underground beliefs. Shadow work is a poetic dance with the delightful and the disturbing. This is your invitation to become curious about what repels you and what draws you in. Let resistance be a cue that something important lies dormant here.

Eventually, an authentic version of the self will emerge with each courageous confrontation as shadow elements lift into the light of the conscious mind. As this happens, you will discover something new about yourself and your potential as old coping mechanisms, unconsciously created to endure difficult life experiences, shift and change. The lies you have been told will come to light. The lies you have said about yourself, your power, and your capacity will meet you as well.

I can teach you, but I cannot understand for you. Ultimately, you will need to walk the dark path alone. Trust me, as terrifying as this first seems, you will soon discover that as you give the parts of yourself that you fear a home, they will no longer consume you.

This home is an intentional writing space that I call a *darkness journal*. Keep reading, and I will teach you how to set up your darkness journal toward the end of this chapter. I have kept a darkness journal for over 15 years. The transformation is unfathomable and unlike anything the 'love and light' and 'good vibes' philosophies had to offer me.

The darkness journal helps draw out afflictions so you can face, heal, and transform them. It sucks to admit we have insecurities; it feels embarrassing to confess our jealousies or disclose to others that we have a vengeful side. It is uncomfortable to sit with ugly and disturbing emotions, and it is normal to feel stuck or unsure where to begin.

Many people fear writing bad things down. They have been conditioned to believe writing out bad things will amplify them like a twisted mantra or vindictive affirmation. This is more bullshit. When you write out the terrible things, you are liberating yourself from them; you are certainly *not* bringing them into your reality like some wretched reverse manifestation.

The shadow work practices offered in this book are designed to work with the psyche, unwinding societal, cultural, and ancestral conditioning. These practices stay true to the origins of Jungian shadow work versus watered-down versions appropriated by various spiritual and personal development teachings, which often disregard the inner workings of the psyche, the unconscious, the personal and collective shadow, and how these seemingly random parts work together.

This book will introduce you to some of these parts, along with others that have been forgotten, abandoned, or simply have not yet had the right conditions to materialize. As the psyche unfurls, numb, disconnected places awaken. As you write in your darkness journal, you will notice the constant tension of concealing what is sacred and the feeling that you must get more comfortable with telling on yourself.

It is critical that while you learn how to write in the darkness journal, you act as if no other eyes will ever take in the horror and delight of your chaotic ramblings. You must ensure you feel safe, so I suggest you keep your darkness journal hidden so it is not mistaken as a regular journal. You may even wish to burn the pages after you finish each entry.

While gathering the bones for this book, a compelling nudge had me pull a few things out of my darkness journal. Some of those fragments are woven in to support the lesson. The darkness journal has helped my clients and students address deep psychic wounds that kept them frozen, invisible, and silent. They recovered from narcissistic abuse, addiction, self-loathing, grief, loss, betrayal, and the most atrocious situations. Many of us have been through unfathomable events and tormented to some degree. We've held secrets and burdens.

Writing in the darkness journal is revealing—we have nowhere to hide when we see what we have bled out on the page. My darkness journal tells stories of countless identities. I look back at words and thoughts written by someone I no longer recognize. The moments of crippling anxiety or depression. Times when I felt helpless or afraid. Stories of failure coupled with the countless ways I numbed or abandoned myself.

Writing in my darkness journal allowed me to retrieve my voice from the gobs of malevolent people and situations that stole it. Every time, I put pen to paper in my darkness journal, an inner door opens. It starts with a forbidden room, locked deep within my mind, yet ends with a cathartic release. A deep wailing cry or a quick exhale, there is never too small of a shift when working with the shadow. I intend this book to expose the forbidden room, giving you the courage to disobey in the best way possible. In the words of Dr. Clarissa Pinkola Estés, "Misbehave with integrity."

For 20 years, I have collected client stories, personal experiences of working with the shadow and darkness, and the mysterious ways the psyche operates on our behalf, moving toward a state of wholeness. Fairy tales helped them emotionally find the way home to themselves. The work must be done with dark, grim, disturbing, intense, and graphic fairy tales. This type of fairy tale contains what is called an initiatory experience. If we look closely, there is always a beginning disguised as an ending, right from the start of the tale, a moment when the main character (protagonist) is faced with an ugly truth and forced out into the harshness of the world (into the dark wood). A form of separation occurs. A devastating truth is that the dangers and hazards often begin in the households we expect to hold us safely.

There are eight fairy tales woven into the chapters, followed by the symbolism of the tale, then a journal process intentionally designed to activate shadow aspects. The best fairy tales stir the cauldron of the mind, open locked doors, cut us into pieces, steal our innocence, and teach us the necessity of entering frightening, dark spaces. They warn us of tricksters and deceit along the path, then soothe our weary souls when we have been fooled or betrayed. Fairy tales teach us how to address abuse, trauma, neglect, and defeat. The medicine is right there for us, embedded in the story, and regardless of the human affliction, we must look at our poisons to find the best remedy for what ails us in psyche and soma.

Modern retellings have been watered down to be more palatable and entertain us instead of deepening into the transformative potential of their inherent archetypal power. We diminished the ugliness of the villains, made the protagonists invincible, and encouraged our young to expect the wicked without being emotionally or psychologically resourced to intuit them. We tell them of the forest, yet their senses are dulled, and without knowing how to survive the terrors and illusions of the forest, they are vulnerable to predators. We shield them from horror, deny their darkness, and avoid things that go bump in the night—yet these monsters are hoping that is exactly what we will do: turn away, look away, and remove the danger from the literature pretend it isn't there. Our innocence pulls us into the dark woods, and our naivety ensures we won't make it out.

Do not dismiss the power of fairy tales. These tales tattle, uncover latent patterns, and reveal the wisdom buried within a wound; they show us what needs to be redeemed, what has been held secret or oppressed. If we look closely enough at the stories, we can gather the parts of us scattered within the tale.

The mind's ability to imagine and create inner images is a potent tool for psychological growth and expansion. The belief that the imagination is childish stems from an overvaluation of logic. Literalization is our need for certainty; we crave certainty over ambiguity. Fairy tales provide the structure and elements that allow the psyche to self-regulate, bypassing the mind's control as we read the story.

We are lost and found in these tales. The tales contain archetypal motifs and repetitive themes that reveal afflictions and inner conflicts through creative and symbolic forms. This directs us to something called the *compensatory nature of the psyche*. This is an innate process that balances psychological disruptions and distortions.

We are as sick as our secrets. Carl Jung, the Swiss psychiatrist who coined the *shadow self*, urged us to confront the darker aspects of the mind. The shadow, a dimension of the psyche, hosts all we loathe, dread, and hate about ourselves. This takes a toll on the body and mind.

The shadow has many functions; one process is reclaiming power from impactful moments. During a trauma or life-changing experience, part of us can appear to be frozen in time. In psychology, we might call this arrested development. Shamanism favors the concept of different aspects of the soul freezing and splitting off, becoming autonomous and difficult to reach. Both speak to the same experience of what can unfold when enduring a traumatic event, impairing the ability to develop emotional maturity. Essentially, we emotionally freeze at the age we experienced the event. This process is a type of regression.

Shadow work and writing in a darkness journal allow us to access these parts that have frozen, splintered off, or disconnected from the larger organizing principle I will refer to as "the self." We begin to understand the age and emotion that cycles through the mind and body, caught in a repetitive, never-ending loop.

Shadow work is a process of discovering and integrating these hidden elements, especially the ones that tell us we are not good enough, that we are flawed or damaged in some way. We give 'place' to our anger and rage, resentment and failures, rejections and denials while simultaneously making room for expansion, healing, connection, and grace.

What we suppress only gains power; therefore, we must make it conscious. This book is a transformational tool to bring hidden aspects to light, to intentionally notice, assimilate, and integrate unconscious energy. When we conceal our terrible moods, vile thoughts, and treacherous feelings, discordant and denied parts continue brewing in our bellies and wombs.

Anatomy of the Shadow

There is no way to tell you exactly what is within shadow, simply because it is not conscious; not everything within shadow is known or knowable. The paradoxical nature of shadow makes it difficult to pin down, yet this is how it operates. To engage with shadow requires trust in psyche (soul) and soma (body). There is a basic structure to the psyche, and understanding the dynamic relationship between these intangible parts orients us to the nature of the shadow.

The psyche is comprised of a persona (the mask we show to the world), an ego complex (the gatekeeper between the conscious and unconscious), the self, the unconscious, and the collective unconscious. The shadow is a psychic field that overlaps the collective and personal unconscious.

All of these aspects interact instinctively and without our conscious control. Beyond function, the complexes act autonomously, as if they have a consciousness beyond the self, a way of operating separate from the mind, behaving on their own accord. If this feels a little complicated, just know the shadow is invisible and contains the magic you seek.

Shadow Myths

A harmful myth perpetuated in various circles is that the shadow is only a warehouse for pain and things we don't like about ourselves. Conversely, some teachings encourage the student to embrace all of who they are. Both ideas are false and dangerous. There are parts of us we can explore and remain curious toward, yet we might benefit from calling ourselves out on something versus embracing it. Boundaries are a must with shadow work, embracing all of who we are or who another is does not create a safe environment and can open the door to harmful behaviors, enabling destructive patterns and cycles. As far as warehousing pain, this is partially true, yet the shadow also contains unmet parts. The gifts, skills, and talents we have yet to discover exist in shadow, the unmanifested potential within, not just the "bad" or unacceptable parts.

How to Create a Darkness Journal

As you read the *Apothecary for the Afflicted*, I recommend keeping a darkness journal to capture thoughts and feelings. Keep it simple; a notebook or journal will do. Through intentional writing exercises, you will start to see your blind spots. Each chapter contains guided prompts for you to respond to in your darkness journal as you read this book.

Shadow work can help you liberate trapped emotions. A darkness journal is a space to engage with the parts of you that you consider ugly and difficult, and the things you find disgusting or disturbing about yourself. By writing in this form, you interact with the journal unconditionally, setting the tone for a surprisingly healing and transformative response called *catharsis*. Catharsis is a Greek word meaning to "purify" or "cleanse." A darkness journal can hold your shadow elements—the parts that are hard to like, let alone love.

Curse, spill the tea, rant, and rave. A darkness journal is a repository that can hold your darkest expressions. As suppressed material arises from the body and psyche, the ego allows more material to move through the threshold from the unconscious into consciousness. This invisible threshold sits between what you know and what you have yet to know.

Writing in the darkness journal starts a process of assimilation, breaking down and understanding the emotions, feelings, or sensations that arise. Next, we can start to integrate the shadow material, transmuting emotion, and stuck energy. This process involves tending to the elements hidden in plain sight—feelings, beliefs, and unprocessed experiences. If you find yourself stuck, blocked, frustrated, or uninspired, you're likely hugging the surface. Sink deeper into the spaces you fear as you write. Do not hold back; do not censor yourself. Let your inner teenager come out. Light and dark are both powerful teachers and catalysts for creative inspiration, only leaning on one dampens the other and creates inner friction. As above, so below. You have been initiated.

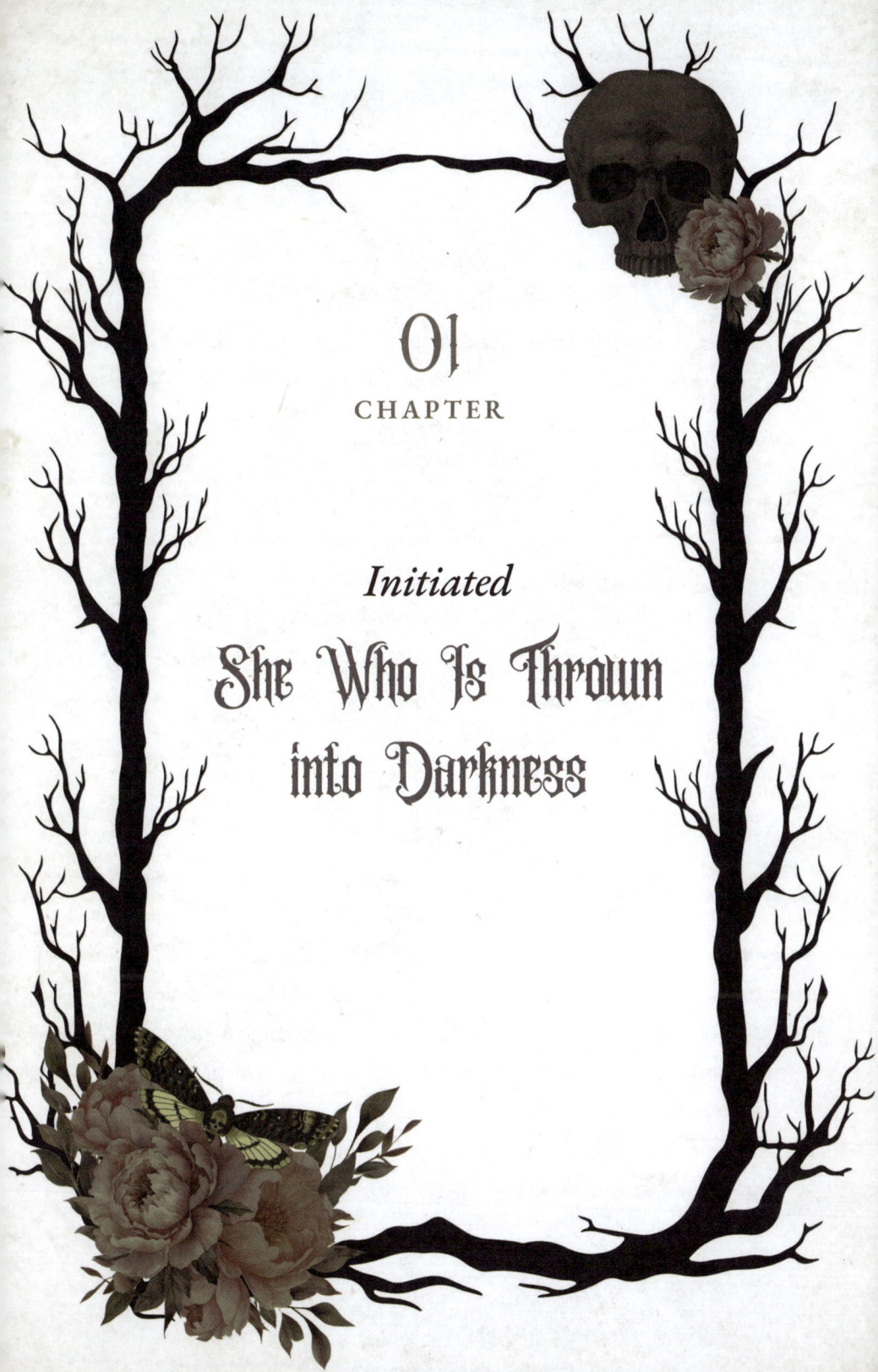

01
CHAPTER

Initiated

She Who Is Thrown into Darkness

"Once upon a time"—these are words we know, somehow, somewhere deep down in our bones, yet we've forgotten their power. These words are an initiation; conscious or not, when we read or utter them, they are an invocation. "Once upon a time" pulls us into the depths, a symbolic space of limitless potential. Depicted in tales as the dark woods, the bottomless ocean, the creepy basement, and the underground cavern, the unconscious is vast without beginning or end. Our first task is to release the idea of the physical location and symbolically open the mind to see these spaces as heavily charged energetic containers. They are places that force us to leave behind comfortable things. Without knowing if we will survive, we are thrust forth, to get moving whether we want to or not.

A beginning is often an initiation disguised as a traumatic or impactful event. Traditional fairy tales reflect a raw power embedded in circumstances of struggle, turmoil, and danger. When we water down our fairy tales, censoring the graphic nature of the narrative, we rob them of their potency. Discomfort with themes of dismemberment, death, and decay are why we have sugarcoated the turbulent nature of being human. Bodies are buried, limbs are torn apart, and blood is spilled. To be fully human means we must get some blood on our hands.

We all eventually go through an initiatory event, a rite of passage that begins with a form of separation; it can be a tragic and chaotic ordeal. An initiation is a psychological movement sometimes accompanied by a physical action, first occurring in adolescence. Initiations are experiences that act as transitional bridges, psychically moving us from one place to another. An initiation may orient around people, roles, or a change in identity. The place does not need to be physical, yet it can include moving out of the childhood home, going to college, getting married, or some other act of separation from the original environment—or, less pleasantly, we are forced against our will, humiliated, violated, and unable to turn away from whatever or whoever stands before us. The separation can sever our trust, rob us of our innocence, destroy our faith, and compromise our loyalties.

In fairy tales, separations occur when the protagonist goes through a painful ordeal. Someone dies, someone betrays her, someone forces her to leave home. Into the dark forest, she goes. Her instincts are challenged and sometimes worn down. She is confronted with a choice, to listen to the small still voice within or fall prey to the louder, external, voice of another.

Sometimes chosen, often not, we find ourselves reluctantly walking a path we feel ill-equipped for. We are humbled and tossed about. We stumble and fall, tumbling down wells, losing the comforts of the homes and people that kept us safe. All that was familiar is stripped away, yet this process is not without purpose. Disorientation is sometimes necessary to quiet the ego and deepen awareness of self; it is often more purposeful than we realize. We are unconscious of our power and are then initiated onto a path, forced to go into the dark forest without knowing what we may come across.

As we walk, bloodied and tired, fears surface, sometimes taking over or consuming us. We fear the monsters we may encounter, and cling to our comforts—until they disappear or are taken. We feel reassurance through the relief of familiarity. We hold fast to the known world with known values, experiences, and expectations. Our egos crave certainty and want it quickly. When things fall apart, the ego begins to grasp. In this moment, we can release our addiction to the light, and begin to question, awaken, and break free from our affinity for positive feelings and familiar experiences.

At such times, we encounter unconscious elements. We try to suppress or deny parts of us for obvious reasons; they can be haunting, relentless, and frightening. We must express pain, suffering, and discomfort by writing in the darkness journal. Hiding pain affirms our belief that it's not safe to acknowledge it, only deepening detrimental patterns. Analyzing shadow involves investigating the elements hidden in plain sight and getting our hands dirty.

In anthropological studies, initiations are considered a rite of passage, honored in ceremony or some form of symbolic gesture that grounds the move into present time, holding the space between who we were and who we are now becoming. These can be difficult times, especially for those of us who encountered initiations early on in adolescence. Puberty is a potent example of this. Without warning the body changes and we move through a threshold that requires aspects of the known identity to dissolve. For some, initiations were ignited through toxic households, forcing the child into the world early, like the protagonist in the fairy tale finding themselves abandoned or orphaned at a young age.

Rejection, abandonment, and betrayal are signposts of initiations, painful catalysts forcing us onto a new path, sometimes willingly, yet often out of necessity.

We are forced to move away from something that is not working: a broken family system, an abusive situation, a pattern of behavior, or a toxic environment.

Rites of passage are often described as ceremonial, sometimes celebrated with guests who are there as a form of support to the individual during this important threshold. These moments include being invited to sit at the 'adults' table or to participate in a cultural ritual or tradition in a way we were not privy to before. For some, it is an age, such as sweet sixteen; for others, maturation or the capacity to expand familial duties or responsibilities.

Some have had to cheer themselves on, without support and with the added stress of trauma or violent opposition. Some challenged the confines of the cages risking their safety. Some fought, clawed, and climbed while holding the anxiety in their bellies with the looming dread of uncertainty as external forces attempted to derail them. Initiations can be painful; therefore, some never answer the calling of a deeper purpose. There are repercussions. It is a risk, and there is no guarantee we will make it out unscathed. No scars, no wisdom.

The dark woods symbolically represent the unconscious; when we are hurled into the unknown. We may endure various levels of emotional, psychological, or physical violence along the way. We can be met with hatred as we turn our attention inward to listen to the small, still voice within. Those who we expect to help us, to nurture us through, may abandon us or act in a way that shocks or surprises us. Initiations can feel lonely and isolating; they dismantle old ways and set the stage for the new, which triggers the ego. The ego may become louder, throw a tantrum, or employ one of its many defenses. We all have ego-defenses; they are automatically activated within certain experiences.

We are haunted and humbled in countless ways. We might feel we are waiting for someone to give us closure, acceptance, or love. Often, we feel unsafe communicating our needs when others cannot hear us. The shadow can reveal what you need to give to yourself because it recognizes the ego's excuses for why you can't do something or move forward. The ego stands between your inadequacy and your forward movement. You are your own medicine.

Intrusive thoughts, macabre interests, and a disturbing imagination are not necessarily valued as they could be. We tend to gravitate toward fluffy manifestation practices and supercharge our focus on good things to co-create our dreams. We must break the terrible stigma that there is only beauty, power, and magic in the positive parts of life, because this leads us to suppress another important part of the personality, my favorite side, the dark side. What we do not give expression to, the body will often release for us. There is deep beauty in learning how to hold your darkness and create a safe and protected practice to unwind intense, ugly, and sometimes ravenous feelings. I call this learning to love our darkness and walking the dark path.

As a deeply intuitive feeling person with a relentless mind, I have intrusive thoughts and have learned to give them a safe place (my darkness journal) to keep them from sabotaging my efforts or infecting other parts of my life. It is a battle of ego. Jungian analysis and my shamanic elders taught me how to transmute darkness, anxiety, and negative repetitive thoughts. We can give space for the elements of the mind, recognizing they are real on some level. The idea is not to literalize these elements but to dissolve the emotional charge they bring so one can extract their hidden meaning.

I have a passion for analyzing terrible dreams and recurrent nightmares. Digging into the emotionally charged narrative of a nightmare, we can discover energy within the menacing imagery that infects our peaceful slumber, a pattern to be decoded and understood. As we choose to stay open and present, the material rises from the unconscious; we then transmute it creatively, so it does not disappear back into the unconscious, which occurs when we ignore it.

Intrusive thoughts and daydreams matter; they reveal where the psyche has a grip on something. The unconscious is generous; it always has abundant material, and our feelings and somatic (body-based) responses are doorways to discovering what is there.

Becoming malleable allows an experience to refine us; this is a departure from our typical desire to understand or control them. Engaging with shadow is not all terrible; it can help us find our way to wholeness. The psychological term for this is *individuation*, the unfolding of life organically according to the soul's directive. In this process, the ego shifts from our prescribed roles, what is acceptable by societal standards, who we should be to who we want to be, what we long for, and our authentic nature. The process of individuation relies on resistance; as we face opposing feelings and situations that create tension, we grow. Each time we face a shadow element, we transmute it, regain power, and reduce the intensity, preventing material from sinking into the unconscious to haunt us later.

Initiations are a type of descent, an emotional experience into the depths brought on by a life event. As we descend, we are humbled by life. There is a downward pull, an undulating motion; it quickly becomes clear we are not who we used to be; the old ways and coping strategies will not serve us in the depths. This is an example of the dark night of the soul. A dark night of the soul can bring us to our knees, hurl us into a spiral, force us to crumble, break down, or send us into an inconsolable rage.

These are difficult times, causing some to give up and leave their bodies. Shame, guilt, and fear are often present in these moments. We are told we fear our light, yet, in my bones, it has always been a fear of my depths. I know I can soar, but getting stuck in a bottomless pit of despair scares me more. My formative years were enmeshed with toxic family dynamics permeated with personality disorders and a host of abusive elements as I met terrible people in my teens. Sorrow was comforting, yet I feared being swallowed by sadness or feeling forever trapped in the underworld (a signpost of depression).

In Greek mythology, the underworld is the realm of Hades, the place where the dead linger. It is not a pleasant pilgrimage; it is arduous at best and filled with trickery and illusion. In the underworld, psychologically, you will not be led by the light; you must learn how to be with the dark, and if you are willing, you will discover the power of darkness.

The archetypal underworld is not the same fearful depiction of hell often told in the West; however, internal turmoil can permeate realms of knowledge and wisdom. The underworld is not only a mythological space but a psychologically dark place containing unconscious elements that can be intense and sometimes difficult to process or reconcile. The acceptance of the underworld can lead to a transformative experience.

Initiations have a way of disrupting our plans to move us toward the deeper impulses of the soul, an often overlooked aspect of shadow work. This requires we cultivate a symbolic understanding of a deep, hidden, psychological process. Transformation is rarely easy. We may feel unequipped and unable to see clearly, during the darkest night or when starting over. The descent is often seen as a psycho-spiritual crisis. There is one who existed before the dark night of the soul, and then there is the one who died and was born again through the ordeal. The one who lived to tell the tale benefits greatly. Initiations may birth new rituals as we move through these dark times. Rituals are not futile; they weave the type of world we wish to wander. Pray, meditate, create, and hold ceremony. Giving big thanks for small moments and using rituals intentionally helps us navigate dark nights and initiations. Rituals help us retrieve our compasses of intuitive discernment and direction.

Reclaiming power from deeply held patterns
liberates the authentic self, giving attention
to the silenced spaces and places within us.
Over the years, my clients have suffered from
addiction, body hatred, self-betrayal, creative
insecurity, loss, incapacitating grief, loneliness,
suicidal ideations, chronic pain, debilitating
fear, depression, and anxiety, as well as varying
expressions of turbulent times in their
encounters with the dark night of the soul.

We all have our burdens, paralyzing and holding us hostage within our minds. Many of us have things we loathe, dread, and hate about ourselves. We encounter unmet spaces and unpleasant faces, and our rendezvous with the shadow are all forms of initiation. The only thing we can take with us is how we choose to view the initiation. To confront shadow is to become conscious of how we see things and to cultivate a form of sight that values symbolism. As we learn to see through illusions, we realize darkness is invisible light and is not to be feared. This is our initiation into the coming chapters.

The Fairy Tale: Vasilisa the Beautiful

On her deathbed, a mother, presses a small doll into her daughter Vasilisa's trembling hands. Her eyes now dim, with a haunting sense of urgency. "Keep it close, child. Hide it well. When the darkness comes—and it will—ask the doll. She will whisper what must be done." Her fingers fall still, yet the weight of her warning hangs in the air as dread rises in Vasilisa's belly.

Vasilisa's world darkens. Her father remarries, bringing home a cruel stepmother and her two spiteful daughters. The warm house grows cold. Vasilisa is wise; she smells all that is rotten, beneath the disingenuous smiles and forced pleasantries.

The girl is singled out, ridiculed, and burdened with impossible chores meant to break her. They resent her beauty, her quiet strength, the light that shines through her presence. They cannot steal it, so it must be destroyed. She does as she is told and only grows more beautiful. The stepmother watches, seething, under her breath cursing Vasilisa's existence in a maniacal tone.

What they don't know is Vasilisa is not alone. In the stillness of the night, she asks the doll for guidance, and is discretely directed. The doll stays hidden helping Vasilisa complete her chores and the impossible tasks.

One night, the stepmother and her daughters intentionally extinguish every light. The house falls into complete darkness. The stepmother demands Vasilisa go alone into the dark forest to fetch fire from the evil witch known as Baba Yaga. The request sends a chill through Vasilisa's bones. Baba Yaga murders and devours children, yet Vasilisa has no choice. Her hands tremble, yet fear is useless here. The forest waits. And so does the witch.

Vasilisa steps into the forest, heart pounding, as the trees close around her. With sweaty palms, she touches her apron and is reminded that she is not alone. Every part of her wants to turn back. Vasilisa's thoughts are interrupted by the awful sight of Baba Yaga's hut. A fence of human skulls, grinning through the dark, their sockets alight with unholy fire.

The door creaks open, revealing the dreadful Baba Yaga. Baba Yaga grins with delight as fresh prey approaches. Vasilisa moves in, one step at a time. Baba Yaga does not deny Vasilisa fire—but she does not give freely.

"You may have fire," Baba Yaga croons, "if you can survive my house." The witch grins, assigning chores beyond human ability, certain she will fail. No one leaves Baba Yaga's hut unscathed. One mistake, and Vasilisa will become her next meal.

The endless and cruel chores continue, each meant to break her. But Vasilisa does as she always has. She listens. She trusts. And the doll guides her night after night. The witch watches, yet the girl does not fail. Baba Yaga's lips curl in irritation, sensing she's being outwitted.

Vasilisa is granted her fire, but not in the way she expects. One night, as the Baba Yaga sleeps, Vasilisa flees into the darkness of the forest— she is lost and overcome with terror. With no direction, tears fall down Vasilisa's cheeks. Aware she has evaded death, she clutches the doll, begging for guidance, "Please tell me what to do."

The doll, answers: "Take a skull from Baba Yaga's fence. Mount it on a stick and carry it home." She does as she is told. The skull's hollow sockets begin to flicker; as a fire burns in the empty eyes, the uncanny light helps her find her way home.

She arrives, and the stepmother and her daughters angrily rip the skull from Vasilisa's hands. Cackling, they bring it inside. The laughter turns to screams as the skull glows, burning the stepsisters, stepmother, and house to the ground. By morning, nothing but smoldering ruins remain.

Vasilisa stands in the ashes, the morning light spilling over her face. She tucks the doll deeper into her pocket. For the first time, it is silent. She no longer needs to ask. She knows the way forward now.

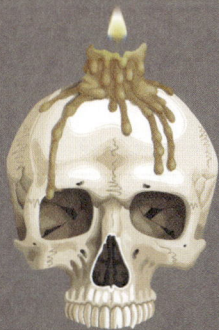

What did you see, sense, or feel as you read Vasilisa the Beautiful?

Check in with your body, go to your darkness journal, and write down any initial impressions, thoughts, or feelings.

Symbolism

Applying this tale to modern afflictions, we can start with the subtle traces of abandonment and betrayal. There are entire books written on the analysis of this fairy tale; this is not a full analysis, only a few critical pieces. The initiation begins as Vasilisa's mother dies. She is instantly torn from the life she knew to a motherless state filled with uncertainty. Here, the ordeals and tasks begin; she is forced into the dark woods to face the unconscious and unrealized parts of herself. The doll represents her intuition; she must never let others on to her gift, her "knowing," and her connection to her instinct. If they know, they will try to steal, destroy, or exploit it. In these situations, we learn to honor our instincts by having them tested.

Monsters and devouring witches cross our paths (Baba Yaga); we give away power and feel lost as we try to find ourselves again. Reading fairy tales opens hidden passageways within the psyche. We are given opportunities to confront the truth, some we wish to escape or avoid. For some, the home was not a safe place for a child, or parents may have been terrible guardians; initiations force us into the harshness of the world.

As we process the rage of abandonment, neglect, and betrayal, we might internalize unfathomable feelings or project them upon others. We may feel as if we will never be good enough, and the ordeals within these initiations can affirm our negative view of self. Sometimes, the child returns to burn the house down.

Confronting disappointment, processing trauma, and sitting with anger allows us to discover new meaning in these experiences. Acknowledging the rage of being initiated into the world before we felt prepared, might lead us to access humble forms of power, intuitive gifts, creative talents, or a new understanding. We can reframe how we view initiatory events, permitting ourselves to feel into the dark, deep, shadow side of the turbulent moments or household we have yet to make peace with. These tales show us the missing pieces, the parts of us we've lost, had taken, or have abandoned along the way. Every time we reread the tale, we receive more and go deeper inward.

Your Turn: Initiated

Not all beginnings are joyful; terrible things happen, and we cannot avoid them and are not meant to. They leave us, lie to us, lie about us, and still, we are expected to carry on. We are left with intrusive thoughts—hiding our suffering, swallowing our seething ruminations. We punish ourselves for the dark thoughts pervading our minds. Instead, we can channel them upon the page; externalize the murderous rage and anger for being thrown to the wolves and thrust upon an unwanted path.

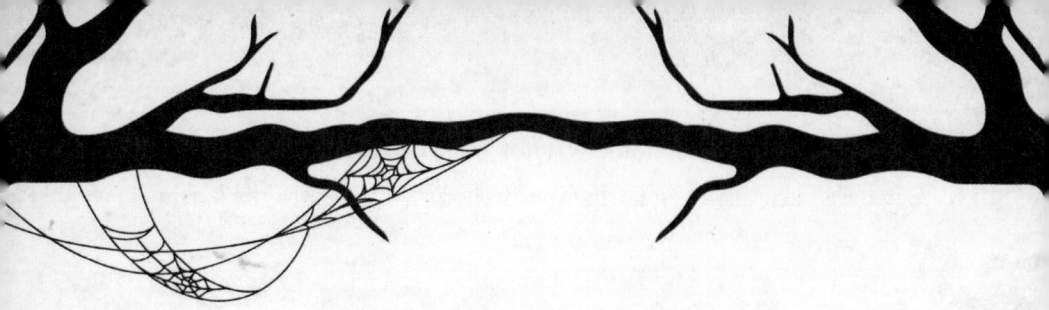

Journal Prompts

What moment(s) felt like an initiation? Describe an experience where you had no choice but to enter the darkness.

Identify your Baba Yaga (a person or event) that forced you to claim your power along the way?

What triggers deeply held feelings of inadequacy; you know, that nagging feeling that says you are not prepared or ready for the task ahead?

Choose one disturbing moment or wretched horrible thing to free write on in your darkness journal, and see what wisdom wants to come out of the wound.

Reflection

Initiation is a psychological and emotional rite of passage, often triggered by trauma or chaos, propelling us into some type of darkness. Fairy tales like *Vasilisa the Beautiful* show us how uncertainty can awaken intuition as we begin confronting shadow material. Even the most painful beginnings are invitations to reclaim lost power. Sit with these ideas, let them stir you, do not rush the memories or moments that are beginning to surface. Instead, channel them here out onto the page...

02

CHAPTER

Inherited

She Who Holds Darkness

As a highly empathic, intuitive child, I was fascinated with other people's basements. Dark, unexplored spaces enthralled me, and my insatiable curiosity toward the hidden dimensions of the mind led to decades of exploring the shadow side of human behavior.

For as long as I can remember, I have held the darkest secrets for others, knowingly and otherwise. Sometimes, this transpired through words spoken to me; other times, this strange phenomenon would occur, as if someone would allow themselves to lose control in my presence so that I could see what was hiding behind their perfectly curated persona. Time and time again, people of all ages would show me who they were behind the facade.

Sometimes our inheritance is being the one who weaves the sacred in the darkest of places. We tend to our fires in secret, behind closed doors, doing the dirty work. We are the ones who pick up the slack, take the high road, and give ourselves in ways others seem to be ill-equipped. An inheritance of conscience, empathy, and empathic gifts presents numerous challenges. My inheritance was a deep knowing that came with not being believed as well as facing the shadow of those who let me see behind their masks. My mother was a wonderful, intuitive, deeply feeling woman. Her conditioning and familial dynamics required her to be the scapegoat, and in many ways, she suffered carrying the expectations of others. I watched closely, and to my surprise ended up similarly carrying the darkness of others. It became clear that I was meant to break this cycle, and it began by learning discernment—to trust what I felt, not what they showed me.

Some people recoiled when they realized I had witnessed part of their shadow, the dark passenger that never leaves. Instead of facing their shadow, they'd flip the script, making me the problem, sidestepping the shame, the fear, the risk of exposure. As a child, it was confusing. I didn't seek out their secrets, but they found me anyway. I could sense things, things people intended to keep hidden, things they feared someone else would discover.

It happened *everywhere*. I'd step into a public bathroom and suddenly a stranger would begin spewing out the details, their mistakes, their deepest regrets. Grown women—complete strangers—would tell me how trapped they felt in their marriages, their voices low, yet directed toward me. In grocery stores, at bus stops, in waiting rooms—people gravitated toward me, unloading the things they couldn't say anywhere else, oblivious to the fact that I was a child.

I felt conflicted about them sharing so openly and vulnerably until I began to understand the hidden pattern in this condition. I believe our secrets and shadow aspects constantly try to move into conscious awareness. This is a self-regulation tactic initiated by the psyche. The psyche moves energy through, mending inner wounds, revealing our darkness so it may be embraced, integrated, and expressed.

Decades of holding darkness, and hearing thousands of gut-wrenching stories taught me valuable lessons about what and how we 'inherit' energy, some of which are patterns we are meant to break. The origin of our wounds sometimes evades us, yet they are clearly seen by the people around us. We think they are invisible, yet others see the behaviors and patterns we try to hide. Sometimes an inheritance requires more than holding secrets and darkness; sometimes it means we must be willing to bring the light, shine the truth, and say the things others refuse to make conscious. We are given the ability to see through illusions, therefore we are the ones who become easy targets for those who are blind to their own afflictions.

In traditional Jungian shadow work, there is a core concept called projection, which is a trickier than most realize. For example, other people can see the rejected or denied aspects of our being better than we can; we may remain under a bit of a spell, entranced by the veil of a projection. We have patterns and cycles operating independently of our awareness, yet others can easily spot them and call them out. These autonomous constructs are psychological and emotional blind spots. We have emotional filters that shield us, and distorted lenses we see through; both can enable our ego defenses (more on this later).

Some of us are highly attuned to the needs of others; some of us have porous boundaries and disappear, never knowing who we are. We may become overwhelmed by someone else's energy or emotions and unconsciously take on their qualities. Darkness unexamined can become poisonous, slowly corroding our identity and purpose, chiseling away personal value, and enabling repetitive spirals of drama and self-destruction.

Blind spots, projections, and ego defenses can sound daunting, as if we are endlessly battling ourselves, unequipped and in the dark. Although initially, it feels like a tireless effort, all these components are part of the individuation process, the self-regulating mechanism of the psyche, constantly moving us back into a state of wholeness over and over again. Occasionally, we need support. One of the reasons our efforts can fall short is psychic fragmentation, also known as soul loss.

The word *lacuna* haunted me the first time I heard it; it refers to an empty space, a gap where something should be, yet it is missing. We know something essential is not present because there is a gap, an empty pocket. We've met people like this; people who demonstrate this unsettling concept. We see it in their eyes. They cause harm intentionally. They purposefully overwhelm others with their darkness as a means of dominance and control. This is evidence of dysregulation, projecting an unmet need onto an unsuspecting person.

Not all monsters come from the unknown. Some birth us, some raise us, and some smile to our faces while they devour us; sometimes, the ones closest to us are the ones who exploit our vulnerabilities. This is disturbing to consider unless it has been your experience. These individuals hide in plain sight, waving to the neighbors and praising in public, while behind closed doors, their darkness reigns. To be on the receiving end of these entanglements is to fight an invisible battle. We get tired. We try our best, but it chips away at the soul and breaks us into pieces.

Psychology and some shamanic perspectives overlap when it comes to these forms of psychic fragmentation, referred to as soul loss. Soul loss reveals itself through a variety of pathological, psychological, and energetic conditions. To walk between worlds is to trust that constructs, ideas, rituals, and practices exist beyond the spaces we comfortably cling to. It is not a literal loss of the soul, but aspects we tuck away to preserve the true self.

Sometimes, parts of us collapse and become consumed or overwhelmed by other parts. Trauma and impactful moments are often responsible for the loss of the soul and the fragmentation within the psyche. Avoiding pain perpetuates physical issues and emotional and spiritual concerns and ailments.

My shadow brimmed with the emotional burden of deeply rooted fears revolving around the loss of control. Fearing a permanent detachment from my true self, I dreaded the moment I would be too far gone, hopelessly trapped in a bottomless void.

Witnessing chronic disempowerment taunted me for decades. Helplessly, I watched as loved ones fell prey to their deeply feeling nature. Suicidal ideations and multiple attempts color my memories. Sitting in hospital rooms, hiding the knives in the home, putting on a brave face, pretending not to see the carnage left behind. One attempt haunts me to this day. Many of us can quickly bring ourselves back into a traumatic event, usually through a quick shift in sensation, memory, scent, or sound. Sometimes, the temperature or change of season can bring it about. I recall the fumes of residual smoke and burnt plastic from an intentionally set fire in our van. It wasn't necessarily this suicide attempt that was the most traumatic, rather the lack of communication, processing of the trauma, and confusion around the events felt like a burden of responsibility. The inheritance of secrets and darkness somehow was passed on to hold yet never be spoken of. The terrible moments we experience teach us about our relationship to suffering and struggle. Some have suffered in unfathomable ways, and this pain leaves an imprint.

Turbulent emotional states were not the only thing infecting my household. Silence oozed through the vents and crept into my bed late at night. In the quiet of the night, I would cry to discharge the emotions and feelings I believed others could not feel.

Inherited moments don't go away; they sit at the edge, patiently waiting for the ego to let them through, and when it does, they make their way into consciousness. Strange sensations and irrational fears are the psyche's attempts to self-regulate, yet the disturbing nature of the sensation and feeling can activate the nervous system and ego to stuff it down.

In what could be a breakthrough moment, we sometimes feel compelled to push away, distract, avoid, or repeat a behavior instead of becoming conscious of the driving force within the behavior. We inherit psychological and energetic traits and perspectives from those near us during our critical formative years. These aspects can be obvious, while others are more obscure, absorbed during physical or emotional proximity to the circumstance. Empaths and highly sensitive people often unconsciously take on the experiences of others, and sometimes, they unconsciously attempt to process them for others. If this resonates on any level, the body may respond to words and ideas regardless of what the memory recalls.

The shadow contains both creative and destructive forces. We may project the dark side of ourselves onto others. Integrating aspects of the shadow has a collective impact beyond the personal and individual psyche. The ripple effect of engaging the shadow cannot be contained; the influence is wide-reaching, immeasurable, and palpable. It is an invisible force with the potential to positively affect cultures, familial patterns, and society. What starts as a personal intention, moves out of the individual realm and into the collective sphere.

There are doorways and latent openings to the shadow hidden in plain sight. Finding them involves intuitively tapping in rather than seeing with the eyes. A shamanic elder helped me turn my intuitive knowing, one of my inheritances, into a gift. Before there was acceptance of my intuitive gifts, there was a confession—I was no longer willing to carry the darkness of others, perpetuating detrimental patterns such as things I was expected to keep quiet. Secrets, burdens, and obligatory relations were no longer welcome.

We take on unspoken rules, traditions, and expectations. Sometimes, things are passed along with good intentions and love, while others demand we carry these inherited experiences by force. I have listened to heartbreaking stories of trauma for decades and have met some of the most resilient people. They have been subjected to terrors beyond my comprehension.

A typical definition of trauma is an event that occurs and is too much, too fast, and too soon for us to emotionally process. Studying tragic stories for two decades revealed the intricate nature of psyche and soma and the mysterious ways the mind and body work to preserve energy and keep us alive. Coping mechanisms and ego defenses become part of our programming, initially to protect, but sometimes operating against our deepest desires and intentions. We become skilled in masking dissociative behaviors, unconscious of the myriad creative ways we avoid being in our bodies.

When deeply divided and dissociated, we are vulnerable to our deeper impulses and shadow material within the unconscious. We may operate through a trauma response, observing ourselves from a distance and acting in ways that appear abhorrent to the outer world while we are numb inside. We all have a unique pathway to healing; mine is sometimes viewed as disturbing or too macabre, yet studying narcissism, psychopathy, and serial killers taught me how to trace the energy of these disturbing figures through film, forensics, and fairy tales. Observing and researching neurosis and disturbing behaviors provided an understanding of aspects potentially lurking within an individual's shadow, deep within the psyche, the dark side many try to act like they don't have.

Before we venture into our next fairy tale, I invite you to take on a new way of navigating darkness, indecision, or struggle. While addressing difficulties, I have observed brave and talented individuals shrink, falling into a trap of speaking to a struggle as if they were helpless, broken, or stuck. Instead of voicing an obstacle with language that enforces powerlessness, I encourage you to try on the terms I have dedicated to this path: sifting and sorting.

Swap out "feeling stuck" for sifting and sorting. Instead of describing the situation as "helpless, out of control, impossible," change the language to match the energetic process. The changes are happening; you just can't see them yet. The help is on the way; it just hasn't arrived yet. The resolution and relief are near; you are just required to remain in this state of dynamic tension for a little longer. When we encounter an ordeal, we are in a state of sifting and sorting. We are learning. We are honing our instincts. We are unwinding old ways, discovering power, and separating via discernment.

Sifting and sorting will come in handy
for most of the tales shared in this book.

Sifting and sorting came about by studying the various tasks and ordeals hidden in the protagonist's struggle in the narrative of a fairy tale. Some impossible tasks are usually given, such as sorting thousands of seeds by dawn, sifting through piles and piles of grain, or locating a needle in a haystack. Ordeals and tasks are a part of many fairy tales; they reflect the psychic process of discernment. You are not inadequate, incapable, or unprepared; you are simply sifting and sorting. We may not like the task at hand, yet some part of the psyche has led us here, to this moment, to this endeavor, to this seemingly impossible feat. Answer the call, and the help will arrive. If only I had counted the times a client or student tearfully whispered, "I didn't ask for this." I held them close, nodded in agreement, and then reminded them that they had everything they needed within to sift and sort their way through difficult and dark nights.

The things we inherit are complex and often paradoxical. Patterns, habits, characteristics, and unique gifts are passed down. We must also learn how to sift and sort through the things we carry for ourselves, others, and our ancestors. Our inheritance can be a gift such as the empathy demonstrated by my mother, or the faith lived out by my father. Some require greater responsibility and discernment. Sifting and sorting is discernment; we can apply discernment to how and when we empathize, share our intuitive *knowings* and whether we take on the emotional burden others refuse to look at.

The Fairy Tale: Cinderella

On her deathbed, pale with her last breath, a mother begs her daughter, Cinderella, to remain kind and loving. It is the final wish spoken before she dies. Cinderella is a sweet girl, generous of heart with a way of bringing light into the darkest of places. She is empathetic and knows the right things to say to put others at ease. She has her mother's good nature and empathic sensitivity.

Her father, grief-blind and absent, remarries too soon—to a woman with two daughters, beautiful in face yet dark of heart. Cinderella quickly senses a shift; a knowing begins to percolate in her heart. Her *knowings* are always

right, yet seldom honored by others so she keeps
her wisdom to herself.

Soon the true colors begin to emerge. The
stepmother could not bear the beauty and grace
of her stepdaughter, Cinderella, constantly
outshining her own daughters. Cinderella
innocently is being who she always has been, yet
her presence stirs their demons. She becomes the
target of those who do not have the courage to
face themselves.

The evil stepmother forces Cinderella to wear
tattered threads and wooden shoes. She does not
hold back and ensures Cinderella has the dirtiest
of the household chores. Saddened by the
endless tasks and desperate for help, Cinderella
goes to visit her mother's grave.

She weeps beside the headstone, begging for
someone to rescue her from this nightmare. She
feels so deeply, and in these moments cannot
make sense of life, nor understand the nature of

cruelty. Why be blessed with a gift of feeling so
deeply, only to have it exploited and used against
her? Out of nowhere, a white dove glides down
and sits on the headstone, reassuring her that
she is capable, that good things will happen, and
that her empathy is a gift. A glimmer of hope is
restored in her heart, so she returns home.

Cinderella continues with her chores, singing
while cleaning and dancing while sweeping.
She daydreams, remembering the dove as she
begins to collect the ash from the fireplace. Her
stepsisters watch on with resentment, taunting,
teasing, and mocking her.

Cinderella feels singled out but does her best
not to succumb to her diminished spirit. They
attempt to strip her of her dignity, laughing
at her and pointing at her disheveled clothing.
Covered in ash and debris, she longs for her
pretty dresses and a time when she was loved, a
time when she felt free to shine her light.

The ugliness of her dress does not compare to the vile words they endlessly spew. Cinderella sees right through them; she sees they are in pain. Her mother taught her that only hurt people could hurt others in this way.

One day, it is announced that the king's son wants to choose a bride, therefore all the maidens are invited to a festival. A chance. A night when every maiden may stand before the prince. Cinderella begs her stepmother to go. Seeing the torment in her eyes as she begs only fills the stepmother with more delight.

The stepmother and her daughters laugh. "A filthy girl in cinders? No prince will look at you." She tosses a bowl of peas into the ashes of the fireplace, laughing her devilish laugh as she taunts Cinderella with the promise that she can go if she picks all the peas out of the ash. They leave her in ruins, taking the finest gowns, the golden carriage, the last remnants of her mother's world. Cinderella stands alone in the dark, then she collapses to the ground, devastated and sad.

She weeps until there are no tears left. Hopeless, she beats her fists onto the earth, angry that she has been left here in this life, abandoned by her mother. At the last moment, doves swoop in to help Cinderella quickly sift and sort the peas from the ash. With joy and excitement, she announces that she has completed the task, only to have the stepmother break her promise, leaving Cinderella behind while she and her nasty daughters leave to attend the festival.

Heartbroken once again, Cinderella cries for help. A dove throws down a beautiful gown and delicate slippers just the right size. A whisper moves through the room. "Be warned, child. The spell breaks at midnight." She does not hesitate. Cinderella rushes and makes it to the feast.

While she attends the festival, her presence captivates the prince who refuses to leave her side. They dance, and for the first time in her life, she is seen. But time is cruel. Cinderella is conflicted, for she knows she must leave before midnight otherwise her gown will return to rags. The first bell chimes. Then another. She runs. She flees through the corridors and the gardens, as the magic dwindles before her eyes. Her foot catches. A slipper falls onto the stone steps. She does not stop. She escapes unnoticed, leaving behind a glass slipper.

The prince is determined to find and marry the mysterious woman, so he goes house to house with the slipper. Days pass. The prince searches. The day arrives when Cinderella's stepsisters get their turn. They try to force the slipper to fit by cutting off toes and heels, but the doves alert the prince to the deception.

The prince offers the glass slipper to Cinderella. Her foot slides with effortless ease into the slipper. It is a perfect fit. The stepmother sees, and her rage erupts like wildfire. She tries to hide Cinderella away, but the girl has spent years learning how to slip through the cracks and survive inside a cage.

Cinderella boldly steps into the light. The stepmother and her daughters watch, their faces twisting in fury, in horror, in something like fear. She marries the prince and returns to her roots. She engages her empathic and tender heart, forgiving her stepsisters. The past burns away behind her. The prince and Cinderella live happily ever after together in the palace. Cinderella does not look back.

What did you see, sense, or feel as you read Cinderella?

Check in with your body, go to your darkness journal, and write down any initial impressions, thoughts, or feelings.

Symbolism

In the beginning, Cinderella does not accept her inheritance of intuition and empathy. She has one of the most important and sacred duties one can have, to tend to the hearth of the home, the fire. Covered in ash, she is close to the remnants of the happenings within the home. If we stay on the surface, we only see the ordeal of having to sift and sort the peas from the ash. If we choose to sink beneath the details, we will discover that only Cinderella can sift and sort, call in support, and get the job done. She can see through the illusions, her sacred sight lets her see the truth in people, and still, we learn the harsh lesson that this is not enough to protect her from their cruelty. To be a fire tender is to bring warmth, light, and soul into a space.

The nasty stepmother and her daughters have no interest in the chores. They elevate themselves, and psychologically, they are inflated and narcissistic. Cinderella is humble with a deep sense of presence. An inflated ego will not involve itself in things it feels are beneath it; we see this with the stepmother and her daughters.

When we are too close, our blind spots keep us from seeing clearly. In this situation, one may become a people pleaser, the first to give credit and the last to receive it. We must stop and question the things we have taken on or inherited. Holding darkness does not require us to abandon ourselves to support another. To do so is not an intentional act; it is one of obligation, a potential shadow of inherited beliefs or behaviors. Empathy is a gift, one we need to develop. Sometimes we learn through the cruelty of others—neglect, manipulation, or avoidance are potent teachers.

Cinderella sifts and sorts in most variations of the tale (some retellings have her on the verge of ending her life) until she consciously chooses to face the impossible task. As Cinderella stays with the tension and surrenders, the doves arrive to help her. We are never alone and must not discount the myriad ways support comes in—including the voice of the soul, a faint echo trying to reach us in the darkest moments.

We may get caught in patterns of self-blame, digging in to find our fault in a matter. Cinderella's empathy is her superpower, yet she finds herself in constant turmoil, ignoring her needs and tending to the home and needs of others. It was not safe to be seen or heard. In some ways, speaking up could make her a target or cause her more suffering.

In the modern day, we might see Cinderella move through a bout of depression, stuck in a toxic family structure, and overwhelmed by the sadness of never being able to be herself. She wished to be close to the same ones who caused her harm; we see her suppress her feelings and battle the despair that comes with being in an abusive, narcissistic relationship. The family dysfunction continues until she breaks down and asks for help; we may attribute this to a dark night of the soul.

On the other side of her ordeals, she could see the villains for who they were, products of unhealed wounds cycling through situations disguised as different faces and places, yet carrying the same toxic energy. Cinderella stopped worrying about the family and found her way to the gathering, the one she had not been invited to. She stopped giving energy to the drama and lies. She took back her power and went to the festival. Cinderella found her authentic expression. Her stepmother and stepsisters never wanted the empowered version of Cinderella; they benefitted from her people-pleasing, and an empowered sense of self would have threatened them. Cinderella stopped believing who they told her she was, broke all the rules, and her rebellion led to victory. Yet none of this occurred without tension, suffering, and a cry for help.

Your Turn: Inherited

Not all traditions are welcome; occasionally, we inherit unprocessed pain, unfinished business, and unconscious burdens as generational wounds seep into present circumstances. As we go through life, we learn how to discern what we keep, what we heal, and what to leave behind. This is why sifting and sorting regarding our inherited ways is crucial. It takes courage to counteract the darkness before it corrupts an innocent heart. We must cut off the toxic supply and stop the damage from accumulating. We reduce our exposure to harmful beliefs and circumstances. Next, we support the affected areas by healing the parts of us that initially accepted the inheritance. We get familiar with our destructive parts and decide we are empowered to transmute darkness and unwanted baggage.

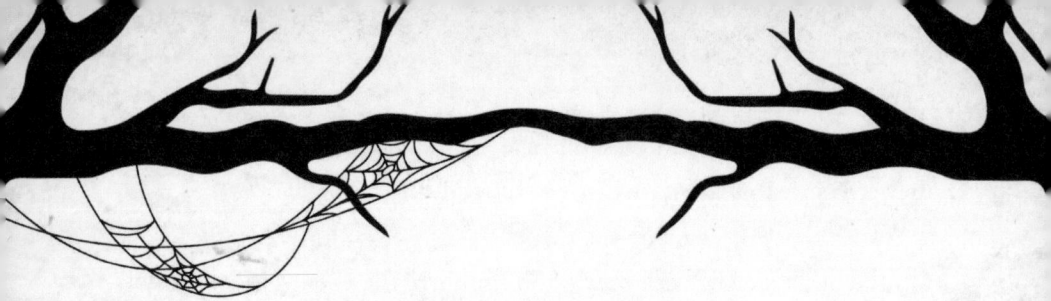

Journal Prompts

What psychological burden (i.e. belief, pattern, or attitude) have you taken on or inherited?

Has your empathy ever felt more like a burden than a gift?

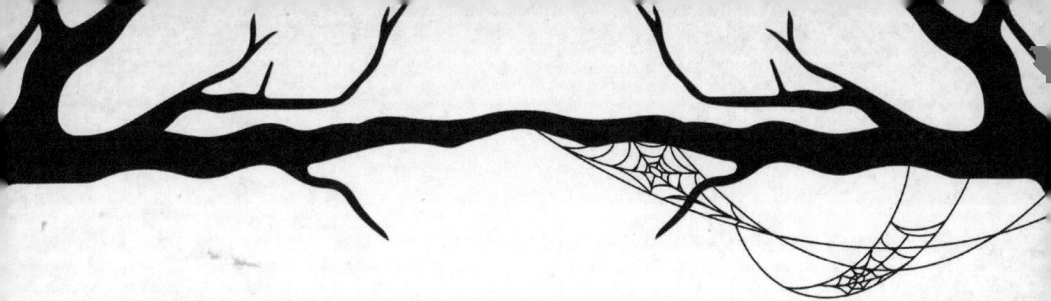

Have you ever been taken advantage of for your kindness and generous heart? Did it change you, and if yes, then how?

～～～～～～～～～～～～～～～～～～～～～～～～～～～～

～～～～～～～～～～～～～～～～～～～～～～～～～～～～

～～～～～～～～～～～～～～～～～～～～～～～～～～～～

～～～～～～～～～～～～～～～～～～～～～～～～～～～～

～～～～～～～～～～～～～～～～～～～～～～～～～～～～

Choose an inherited trait/energy/issue/cycle to free write on in your darkness journal, and see what wisdom wants to come out of the wound.

～～～～～～～～～～～～～～～～～～～～～～～～～～～～

～～～～～～～～～～～～～～～～～～～～～～～～～～～～

～～～～～～～～～～～～～～～～～～～～～～～～～～～～

～～～～～～～～～～～～～～～～～～～～～～～～～～～～

～～～～～～～～～～～～～～～～～～～～～～～～～～～～

Reflection

In this chapter, we considered the things we inherit—not just traditions or qualities, but psychological burdens, ancestral trauma, and energetic patterns passed down through family and experience. *Cinderella* emphasized how empathy and intuition can both feel like a gift or a curse when we lack discernment. Healing begins with confronting what we've inherited, consciously choosing what to keep, and sifting and sorting through what must be released. Tune in, notice what is rising up, try to capture the essence and write about it here...

03

CHAPTER

Haunted

She Who Knows Secrets

Ghosts are portrayed as shadowy figures with unfinished business, believed to be the souls of the deceased, returned to haunt the living. We are haunted by guilt, regret, ancestral burdens, things we refuse to see, sense, or feel—all forms of unfinished business. Sometimes we are haunted by events that another has refused to acknowledge, and we carry the responsibility to transmute the energy.

Perspective determines how and what haunts us. Hauntings are often evidence of the psyche's guidance. Once we remove fear or discomfort, we can discern the hidden ghosts that haunt us. We can trace them back to thoughts, feelings, behaviors, and incomplete conditions. To face what haunts us requires us to stay open. There is no singular path to uncover our ghosts, not only one way to exorcise our disturbances.

This is why I use psychological thrillers and horror movies to help people process emotional turmoil, to give a story or a physical representation of something lacking form within the psyche. Until the energy is free to move, it is sensed as an ominous irritant that pesters or festers until given an outlet. If we cannot locate the origin of a feeling or pattern, the expression may be thwarted. The emotion or energy is bound up until we intentionally create an outlet or bring closure.

The task requires trusting intuitive impulses, subtle thoughts, and seemingly random feelings. Intuition is essential, and we must learn to trust that we have invisible processes governed by a mysterious organizing principle called the "self" within the psyche. All this unfolds automatically as the self finds and collects various pieces, the parts we have severed or been emotionally butchered by others.

> We are not always given the full details, so we must trust the psyche's process as it moves us toward wholeness. Aspects within shadows begin to rise, ascending to meet the ego. We receive this as darkness (unknown) moving to light (known) consciousness; we then assimilate and transform the energy. Self-trust is essential, and unsettling images, thoughts, feelings, and sensations may be a part of this process.

Those drawn to true crime, horror, or psychological thrillers are not deeply disturbed. They are not bad people; they are not lowering their vibration or inviting chaos into their lives by consuming these types of films or media. Often, they are highly sensitive individuals who feel deeply; their empathic gifts make them incredible investigators, reporters, storytellers, and warriors for justice.

Many of my clients are these types of people. They find common elements and string them together, a thread connecting one detail to the next, revealing a hidden pattern or connection. Sometimes, a movie can unlock some stored energy within the viewer, so much that it can take weeks to understand and integrate. Disturbing feelings are amplified by the film's imagery, sounds, and tone in this setting. Experiences do not always move through us in a methodical format. Sometimes, a scent, image, song, or feeling unlocks a door long ago locked. If we are willing (and feel safe), we can tend to the sensory input and use it as a form of information to help us understand what anxiety is trying to convey, perhaps revealing the energy that haunts us.

If something scares you, makes you uneasy, feels too edgy, causes a sense of dread, or leaves you unsettled, wonder why. Instead of assuming it is the film or content, adopt a symbolic attitude and become curious about why you are captivated or repulsed by the content. Each movie holds archetypal value and meaning based on the inner movement of your unique processes. Regardless of what the film was created to express, there are always other psychological elements at work within you as an observer. Not everything is about unresolved trauma, but when it is, psychological thrillers are valuable tools for helping you process things you cannot name, describe, or remember for a variety of reasons. You can tell if there is unfinished business for you in the experience by asking yourself a straightforward question—does this material have an emotional charge to it?

Children know when a heated argument has occurred; they feel it. They also sense when the parent turns away to hide emotion by covering it with a smile. The child feels the latent emotion as it lingers in the air. The fighting stops, but the emotions continue circulating through the child's body. The child may freeze, run away, or get agitated; the child might get scared or sad or project emotion onto a parent. There are countless responses, and deeply sensitive children will take on the emotional burden and internalize the experience to diffuse the emotion, so it feels better. Children are not always taught how to stabilize emotions or regulate the nervous system. Unfortunately, these experiences leave an impression; the emotional haunting of unresolved experiences follows us from childhood into adulthood.

We are given experiences that do not make sense to the logical mind, so we learn to feel our way through. The issue is that we do not trust ourselves; we trust the ones telling us how things are. We learn to make ourselves wrong. We believe others and begin lying to ourselves.

In every lie we tell ourselves, there is a moment, an intuitive reaction, a signal we cannot hide from ourselves. We can ignore it, as many do, using the ego to justify the lie. Yet that feeling will call you to it every time, and eventually, it will bury itself deep within the mind or body until one day, when least expected, it will emerge. This can become the source of anxiety, depression, or sadness. Not the act of lying itself but the inability to understand which part of us was capable of lying; maybe we even needed the lie to keep a hidden defense operating. We become masterful at cutting ourselves off from other spaces within the mind, yet they still exist and contribute to our hauntings.

We sense warmth, the same as we sense distance. When we are close to safe, warm people, we cannot help but unfurl like a frond on a fern. Oppositional to the opening, when we encounter deception or

manipulation, parts of us begin to pull back and retreat, an instinctive warning system. Yet our unmet needs win this battle until we develop a healthy ego, the part of us that helps us establish and uphold boundaries.

Studying darkness, shadow, and psychopathy has given me this gift. Through the painful undermining presence of manipulation disguised as love, I learned how to cut to the truth. Highly sensitive and empathic people sense and know things that others may not recognize. Those drawn to explore the shadow are likely those who see patterns, recognize illusions, and look for the symbolic nature of a situation or experience. Ignoring the shadow dimension of human behavior perpetuates an unhealthy one-sided affinity for all we deem holy and good. This can create psychic fragmentation, splitting, and soul loss.

Suppression is an internal move to control, push down, deny, and dispel challenging aspects and emotions. All we are unwilling to see in ourselves remains in the body. These elements do not dissolve once we withdraw our attention; the unprocessed thoughts, feelings, and impulses are pushed back into the unconscious. When we suppress the material, it contributes to the formation of a complex. A complex is an energetic trigger that sits in the shadow. It is made of intricate motifs. These motifs repeat themselves. They linger and haunt us like ghosts. They keep us in limbo, between worlds.

Symptoms, feelings, and relentless patterns all have an archetypal component, a buried story within the center, a core wound protected by energetic layers. In awe, I've observed and held space for women to unwind suppressed emotions stored in the body, specifically in the bowels and womb, as they released emotions from the dark spaces of the body. Many carried unexpressed rage, guilt, and shame. Finding beauty in darkness allows us to attune to our bodies and the land, the places we reside and call home. What once haunted us now begins to guide us. Our ghosts can become our wise counsel, like a supportive ancestor.

We cannot transmute what we are not willing to witness. Nightmares, resistance, and the body all point to the buried consciousness, darkness as a form of invisible light. We are suppressing by intentionally stifling unmet needs and unfelt feelings. The shadow contains these suppressed aspects until they are dealt with. Consciously or not, they return to haunt us in other forms. The shadow gives us signals, intuitively moving us toward healing. Many are haunted by pain and have yet to experience their power to reclaim the pieces of their past and potential for the future. Womb and bowels are viewed as body-based 'locations'; these vessels contain vital processes, allowing for the creation and assimilation of life. We are born of the womb and process life through the bowels; in darkness, matter contains an essence of inherent consciousness.

Women carry darkness for the collective. Our roots go into the earth, the soil the dark place of deep germination, a womblike quality found in nature. The bowels are a symbolic cauldron, a sacred container, and an underworld motif. Within the bowels, a breakdown occurs as part of digestion. Emotionally, we may consider how we digest occurrences and circumstances in life. In some traditions, the bowels are considered a sacred place of deep knowing and intuition.

The underworld is a shadow expression of 'place' and cautions that avoiding a symbolic attitude and overly favoring a rational perspective destroys creativity. Honoring deeply held grief, ceremonies rooted in release and forgiveness can mobilize stored energy through literal and symbolic gestures of letting go. Healing my womb and my digestive system (bowels) meant learning to be with the feared places within me and releasing all that kept me from being my authentic self. I felt haunted.

Nature can help facilitate spontaneous processes as we unburden our hearts and bodies. I sat with my rage in a canyon, and there were signs that recovery was well underway after a devastating fire burned through the region. Witnessing the destruction, I sobbed, overwhelmed by the damage. This place, badly burned due to human interference and negligence (a tossed cigarette), broke me open. Deeply held anger and rage poured out as I recalled moments when another's carelessness had burned me. The land was healing, and this evidence of growth reminded me that I, too, was recovering.

Marked and scarred by fire, black charring blended with greenery revealed how a space could be simultaneously healing and whole. The fire element and I had a tumultuous relationship; my mind flooded with searing moments. Then my attention shifted to the fresh growth, the thriving plants and trees, tiny buds springing out of the ground. I sensed the resiliency of this beautiful place and carried the feelings back to my body. If the earth could be this trusting to grow here and show its beauty again, I could do the same. I was overwhelmed by how 'held' I felt, nurtured by this space, like an endless womb. The canyon contained it all, and I felt my body like a magnet on the earth. It felt ceremonious to be held by the earth. My nightmares once consisted of fires and tsunamis; both have yet to return since I learned to be with my rage and to appreciate my macabre, weird, wild ways.

We can tend to our inner spaces with the support of nature as we learn to feel at home with her and our bodies, engaging with body and place. Sitting in overgrown spaces reminds us of the places left wild within us—untouched by life experiences, unruly, perhaps a bit feral. Dimly lit barren spaces, empty. Those places where nothing but the wind is present. Emptiness is the illusion. Each space is a vessel, a containing space ripe with potential to hold and allow ideas to move in, a womb germinating in its right time, offering rest and reprieve. We project upon the land and see what we want to see, and other times, we are attuned—sensing feeling, knowing something is emerging, wanting to be seen and recognized by us. Recognizing that we can heal and recover *and* are still whole is transformative.

Unconscious material may resurface as dreams, symptoms, repetitive patterns, compulsions, or impulsive behaviors. The witch hunts are an example of the oppression of the feminine and how the feminine became a scapegoat for the collective. Another form of oppression can be traced to the roots of hysteria. Hysteria is an example of 'evil' projected upon women; as the first mental disorder, hysteria initially fell under either a scientific or demonological perspective. There's a tendency to label distasteful or unfathomable subject matter as evil. Women underwent excruciating, abhorrent rituals. Some were punished and purified with fire, which was believed to be a cure. Facing these horrors requires us to tend to the shadow; only then can we unveil the power of our darkness, our instinctual nature.

In fairy tales, hauntings are sometimes represented by the spirit of a human or animal trying to communicate with the living. The protagonist can be seen trying to engage with the figure, or he or she may run away. Sometimes, an inanimate object, such as a pair of shoes, will come to life by a ghost animating the object to communicate information to the living. The haunted energy may take over a home, person, or situation; there is an attempt by the natural world to call out deception or reveal a secret. We sense something is off but this intuitive insight is usually dismissed in the tale, distracting the protagonist, and separating them from their power, sense of agency, or instinct.

Fairy tales have a way of exaggerating our human conditions, using various elements to convey information that might seem supernatural, fictitious, or completely absurd. A symbolic eye takes time to cultivate as we learn to tamper down the part of us that tries to dismiss the circumstance or downplay its significance. If we recall, fairy tales help us observe parts of the shadow. We can trace the unconscious aspects personified by the characters in the tales. The closer we look symbolically, the more is revealed, uncovering lessons, and learning about ourselves from within the framework of these seemingly innocent stories. Sometimes, they remind us that into forbidden places we must go.

The Fairy Tale: Bluebeard

Bluebeard was a wealthy man with an ugly and unnatural presence. His beard was strange, an off-putting hue of blue. Even his wealth was not enough to cover the deeply unsettling force that operated within him. Everyone felt it and tried to steer clear. He was notorious for his atrocious behavior toward his countless wives, all of whom disappeared without a trace; and worse, they vanished without anyone trying to find them— their fates completely unknown.

Still, he married again to the youngest of several siblings. They were all frightened by his appearance and aware of his wicked ways. All but the youngest seemed to react in horror to his features. She was reluctant and sensed something sinister behind his smile, but she gave in to the expectation of societal pressure. The clock was ticking; she wanted to be married by now. She overlooked the warnings, dampened the whisper of her intuition, and followed what she thought was her heart.

Upon arriving at his vast estate, Bluebeard hands his new bride the keys to the home: seven keys for seven rooms. She can come and go as she pleases, with *six* rooms to freely explore, but she is forbidden to enter the seventh door. She sees something deviant in his eyes as he leans in with his hot breath, solidifying the fear rising in her belly. She nods in agreement that she must never enter that forbidden room.

Soon after, Bluebeard must attend a business meeting, leaving his new wife home alone. At first, she is content and explores the house, moving from one room to another. Yet it doesn't take long for the curiosity to churn. She does her best to push it down and busies herself with something else, but she begins to ruminate: what would he do if she were to betray him?

Though her mind spins and wanders, her feet lead her to the forbidden door. She cannot stand this unsettled feeling, antsy and without relief. She knows on some level she has already made up her mind. Each moment wears down her resistance. Just as she hits her edge and can no longer endure the rising curiosity, the key begins to burn in her hand.

The compulsion takes over. She is overcome with the urge and thrusts the key into the locked door. There is no going back. The door swings open, and before she can take in the enormity of the horrors before her, blood begins to pour from the walls. The decaying corpses of Bluebeard's previous wives are piled on the floor; their bodies stacked like discarded objects. Scattered bones and flesh construct the nightmare of this horrendous scene. His murdered wives' lifeless bodies speak volumes; although they were silenced, the room loudly shouts out the monstrous truth. Blood covers the walls and pools on the floor.

Frightened and frozen in terror, the new wife drops the key into one of the pools of blood. The key comes alive and soaks in the crimson liquid. Forever haunted, the key tells her secret, openly displaying her deceit.

She recoils in disbelief and frantically attempts to wipe the blood from the key, yet the blood remains. Desperate, she rubs her hands raw scrubbing the key in hot water. Her eyes widen as the key repels the soapy liquid. Her heart sinks as she hears the familiar sound of heavy footsteps on the walkway. He is home.

Bluebeard returns. Before she can inquire about his trip, he asks for the keys. She hesitates and sheepishly smiles while handing them back,

hoping the bloody key will go unnoticed. His
breath quickens; he grunts an unnatural sound.

Fear slowly grips her entire body from head to
toe as a wave of panic floods her being. It is clear
he knows he has been betrayed. Before she can
think he has her by the throat, shaking her while
threatening to kill her for betraying his only
wish. His brute force overpowers her. She feels
the life slipping from her as she mentally tries to
escape this dire circumstance. He barely lets up
enough for her to get the words out. Her blood
would soon join the others.

She begs for a moment, just one moment so
she can prepare for her death. She wants time
to pray, to prepare her soul for death. In a rare
act of compliance, he gives it to her. He has not
softened; it simply elongates the pleasure he feels
in watching her suffer, knowing her life is near
its end. His pleasure is drawn from the fear that
looms in the air.

She kneels, hands trembling not in prayer, but in silent, frantic summoning. She did not pray for salvation; she prayed for her brothers. Just as Bluebeard is about to kill her, footsteps thunder outside. The door bursts open—her brothers rush in, knives in hand, sharp metal glinting in the light.

They kill the murderous tyrant. She was the last wife, the only one who lived. And now, the house—the terrible, chamber of horrors— was hers. She inherits the house and all of Bluebeard's riches. Still warm from his hands, the keys rest in her palm, no longer bloody but shiny, clean, and exorcised.

*What did you see, sense, or
feel as you read Bluebeard?*

Check in with your body, go to your darkness journal, and write down
any initial impressions, thoughts, or feelings.

Symbolism

Bluebeard can be viewed as the shadow, the darker destructive elements
of the psyche, the turbulent uncertainty of individuation. Our own
shadow and the shadows of others haunt everyone involved. We are
forced to contend with the shadow, denying obvious and blatant issues.
Everyone is aware of Bluebeard's terrible reputation, yet he's never held
accountable and continuously gets away with murder.

No one looks for the disappearing wives. Narcissists and psychopaths
leave evidence of their destruction, usually disoriented and defeated
people who are left trying to heal from the aftermath. The bride
continuously dismisses her instincts. She opts into a marriage to appease
a societal expectation, blind to the patterns she is committing herself to,
legally, but more importantly emotionally and energetically.

We become aware of the forbidden room, a sign that we are not to enter,
explore, or look any closer. We may all have spaces like this within us, the
things that haunt us, memories we suppress, or secrets we are forbidden

to expose, even though they may be destructive and damaging. This keeps one from expressing emotions, locking them away until they erupt into consciousness in another form. Migraines, addictions, crippling anxiety, avoidant behaviors, and a mountain of debt are only a few of the countless symptoms trying to show us that our attempts at hiding the skeletons are not working. We all have skeletons; some have been given to us, some passed on, and some require our participation to keep them secure and hidden.

When the bride opens the door, the secrets overwhelm her. She can't hide from Bluebeard's horrendous past. Once we open the door, all is exposed. No longer shielded from the horrors or tragic moments, the blood is unavoidable and speaks to the countless lives lost, the voices silenced and suppressed. Blood can reflect a sacrifice or direct us to an inescapable truth that must be confronted, both are a sign that the heroine has crossed a threshold of knowledge and cannot go back to *not knowing*.

There are consequences to rejecting our intuitive knowing, and our choices in these moments can haunt us. The bride unlocking the forbidden room symbolizes the need to confront the unknown. When we are forbidden to do something, there's an energy that begins to build. Some sense fear, validating a need to keep that door closed, while others are led by impulse or curiosity, unable to resist the urge to enter the room. The bride's curiosity leads her to face the horrors, which become a catalyst for growth.

The blood cannot be washed off the key, symbolizing something that needs to be revealed. The key haunts the bride, refusing to conceal what she wishes to hide. Unconscious elements have come forward and been made conscious; we can't unsee what we've seen. What is now conscious cannot revert to a former state of naivete. We don't have the luxury of going back in time. The blood on the key, just like a stain, it has left its mark, impacting our consciousness. It is a haunting that is in service to growth, bringing the shadows into the light.

In many versions of the tale, the young wife is saved by her brothers as Bluebeard is about to kill her, which could symbolize the intervention of more balanced psychic forces to restore harmony and order.

An authentic rescue comes from our intentional actions: acknowledging the horrors, facing the consequences of curiosity, and ultimately surviving an encounter with the shadow. *Bluebeard* cautions us about avoidance while requiring us to face our inner darkness or be honest about what we see in another. This tale shows what happens when shadow material is assimilated and then integrated.

Your Turn: Haunted

Some moments haunt us, and others humble us. Each time we sit with our ghosts, they become our ancestors, imbuing wisdom through the same thoughts, feelings, and presence that once caused discomfort. To be haunted is to be human; our great task is to experience life fully, feeling, assimilating, and integrating as we move into the next experience.

When we are haunted, we have yet to discover the wisdom within the circumstance. See through the ghost, and you will discover a hidden power. It's your turn to reflect on the ideas and themes of this chapter, then use the following prompts to go further into the depths.

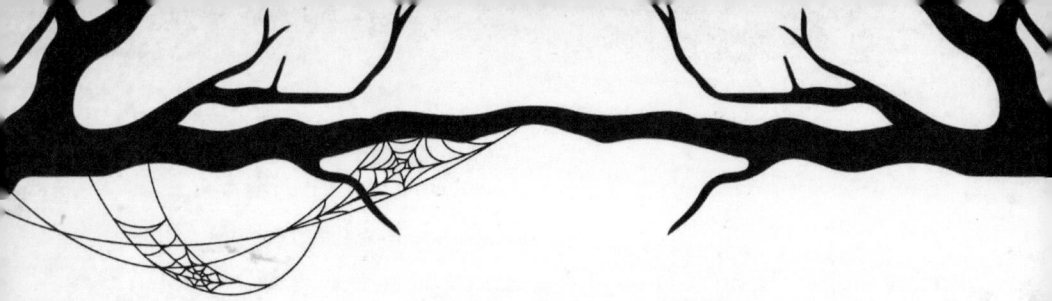

Journal Prompts

What haunts you in body, mind, or soul? Have you ever been haunted by something someone else has done?

~~~~~~

~~~~~~

~~~~~~

~~~~~~

~~~~~~

What wakes you in the night and won't let you be?

~~~~~~

~~~~~~

~~~~~~

~~~~~~

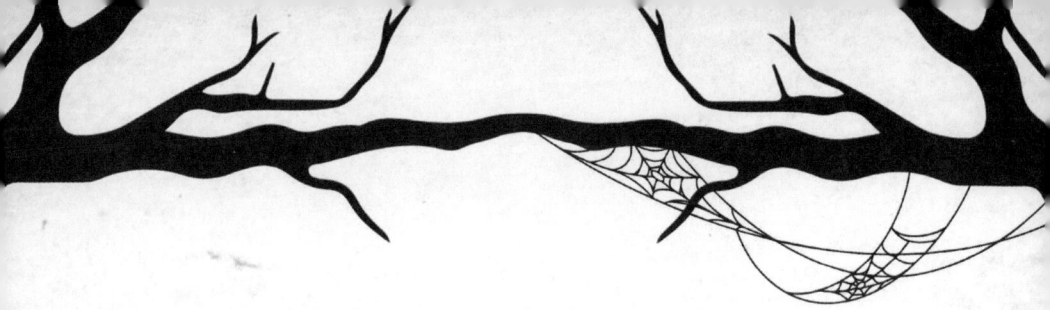

Call out your ghosts by name. Who and what are they? What do you need to put them to rest?

~~~~~~

~~~~~~

~~~~~~

~~~~~~

~~~~~~

Choose to face something that feels unfinished, and free write on it in your darkness journal; see what wisdom wants to come out of the wound.

~~~~~~

~~~~~~

~~~~~~

~~~~~~

~~~~~~

Reflection

In this chapter, we thought about our
unfinished business, the things that haunt
us both psychologically and emotionally.
Bluebeard taught us that what we avoid or
hide will eventually come out of the closet,
forcing us to look closer at what is ready to be
integrated. What haunts us holds insight, and
facing our ghosts with honesty and curiosity
transforms our ghosts into ancestors. Notice
what lingers in body or mind, do your best
to honor it and get it out onto the page...

04
CHAPTER

Dismembered

She Who Is
In Pieces

Sometimes, we must separate from something to see it more clearly. The psyche is born whole; there is interconnectedness and a state of wholeness before the ego develops. This is called a preconscious state of wholeness. It is the original condition of the psyche: the *unio naturalis*. As the ego forms, our wholeness is lost. We move through impactful moments and traumatic situations. We are betrayed, rejected, abandoned, violated, humiliated, or experience a combination of them over time.

Our return to wholeness requires great sacrifice, the dismemberment of the ego (a division of parts) as it knows itself to be—this is individuation, a restoration of connection with the self, nature, and all that is essential beyond materialistic desire. An ego that is convinced that it is the center of consciousness will fight the unconscious. We must endure moments of being pulled apart, a psychological dismemberment, a separation that allows us to be put back together again in a new form.

We experience dismemberment when we are separated from our instincts and intuition. We also experience it as the ego is transformed. Old structures crumble and birth a new and more conscious ego. In fairy tales, *mortificatio* is the death of the king, the dominant ruling principle, the ego. This version of the ego must die, so it is no longer the center of consciousness; it then creates room for the psyche to reorganize around the authentic self.

The ego can only see through a narrowed lens, a fragment of what is possible. Putting ourselves back together again happens each time we face a core wound, each time we choose ourselves, and each time a boundary is held. All these things help us build inner ego strength to handle external factors such as tension, resistance, and struggle. The dark night of the soul is sometimes marked by a stripping away of everything familiar and safe. These moments activate and stir the cauldron of the human psyche.

The dark night of the soul can feel like torture, filled with suffering and deep despair. We are given insight into the current state of the ego. The ego will fight and resist as it is deconstructed and dismembered; sometimes this resistance prolongs the process and makes things worse. We have the opportunity here to learn how to surrender, over and over.

For some, sanctuary is not found in the home, our initial place of dwelling, the place where we were raised. Depending on our family of origin, the home can be a source of distress rather than a safe container protecting us from the outer world. There is often a time in a young girl's life when the world is devastatingly disenchanted, when people disappoint, harm, neglect, or abandon; the cold, rigid, manufactured, and conditioned truth of reality sets in. And still, nature holds space as we gather the broken pieces of a shattered reality, mothering us as we mend ourselves.

When we forget what nurtures us and skip our rituals, we may default into old patterns and cycles, spiraling into emotional states we fought to overcome. Spiraling can signal that we are building up unexpressed feelings and emotions and holding other people's stuff if we continue to compartmentalize. Healing happens in safe spaces with people who can witness us as we learn to hold the various parts of who we are.

During my dark night, one of my dear elders, a powerful mentor, guided me through a shamanic process of dismemberment and reconstruction. Muscle, flesh, and bone are deconstructed with the help of a raven or vulture through a deep meditative journey, signifying the removal of the old and deadened aspects, then offering the dead up to the higher powers for renewal. The process took months to recover from and integrate into daily life. An integration occurs as the parts are combined to form a new structure and reconnect with the depths.

During this process, we move into a state of being that merges spirit and matter; the wisdom now lives in the bones. The heaviness of the dark night of the soul shifts, and the soul is integrated and reunited with the body. The split heals and wholeness returns. I began to see evidence of wholeness, finding myself animated and joyful again, excited to wander in the woods and write down my daily insights, engaged with the magic and beauty of the natural world. A deeper, intricately woven web of connection emerged, and I knew without a doubt that I belonged to it.

Wholeness expands our capacity to be with the great mystery, the divine, the numinous, to open our eyes and hearts to the auspicious and generous nature of the cosmos. We uncover more of our soulful and authentic light by learning to be with our darkness. At first, embracing the depths is uncomfortable before opening to the numinosity of it all. Blindly flying toward the light, we normalize our disoriented state while the soul patiently resides in the background. Each time we attempt to outrun the shadow, we stunt our growth, inhibiting the courage that awaits us in the depths.

The ego is vital in liberating the soul from the instincts and the unconscious, separating us from our appetites and desires since complexes, instincts, and appetites drown out the soul's voice. When we continue to repress the qualities and refuse to see, unconscious patterns can wreak havoc and destruction upon our lives. The denial of these shadow qualities sets the tone for an eruption. As we turn to face the things that scare us, we unwind, moving through new thresholds. For some, this can be a slow and torturous unveiling.

As we confront ourselves and are taken apart, the relationship between body and mind shifts, altering the relationship with our ancestors, going back in time and forward for future generations. Turbulent times offer the chance to integrate multiple parts, mending a fragmentary perspective as the mind tries to find a relationship between its separate parts, a spontaneous facilitation of individuation.

Individuation is a process of becoming whole, the unfolding of self through the healing of psychic fragmentation. As our deepest drives emerge, a cyclical integration process and movement toward psychic wholeness naturally occurs. We cannot experience psychic wholeness while avoiding darkness or suppressing destructive forces individually or collectively. This liberation of energy becomes possible with the confrontation of darkness and the willingness to open the closet and get to know the skeletons.

As a child, I was an old soul; everything seemed to contain profound meaning. Surface-level conversing was never appealing, and I loathed being stuck in soulless dialogue. I sought the hidden treasures buried within people, places, and nature. In adolescence, this was a blessing, but as I matured, this quality led me into dangerous situations, and I was emotionally torn apart.

The individuation process can be viewed as the reclamation of self, bridging childhood with lessons and integrated ways of being and re-enchanting the world while grounding into a healthier state of presence gleaned later in life. Life is a creative attempt at weaving a psychological, cosmological, and biographical tapestry. The threads include the birth of an authentic self as the unfolding psyche moves through the evolutionary process of individuation conveyed through various moments and memories.

Repetitive themes rose to consciousness, forming the bones of my past: initiation, intoxication, incubation, and integration. The larger tapestry comes to life by observing psychological and mythical moments tucked within the biographical experience translated through a few decades of intense shadow work. My shadow contains traces of a part of self that loves the depths and avoids the monotony of surface-level encounters. Individuation can be viewed as an unfolding through reflections, revealing latent patterns, and offering insight into the intricate ways the soul speaks through the stars to orient oneself within life and the cosmos purposefully.

I have been known to give clients and students homework that would probably be shocking for those who only focus on love and light and do not have a relationship with darkness or shadow. I recommend clients watch psychological thrillers and take notes on the various ways they viscerally respond to the imagery, noticing somatic sensations and discomfort. I have given clients homework to research certain serial killers based on the psychological splitting I notice in their patterns. Certain individuals demonstrate the repressed quality my client is stuck exploring, and by discovering the projections placed on these intense figures, they can learn something about themselves.

As unconventional and disturbing as this may seem, consider that you have been caught in a feedback loop most of your life, and your pattern includes people-pleasing, always doing the right thing, and carrying the emotional burden of always being the responsible one. Then, a murderer appears in your dreams, or you are the murderer in the dream. These experiences reflect the psyche borrowing someone or something else to show you what has been cut off, what is vulnerable, and what part of you is dying or needs to be killed off. Ignoring the dream, the intrusive thoughts, and the energy of the complex is like trying to use all your effort and energy to push things down that refuse to remain hidden.

More often than I can count, a client has reluctantly shared these horrific and terrible nightmares, only to discover there was a hidden language and symbolism buried within the dream. They needed a safe person to reveal these elements to, someone to help decode them. Nightmares and dreams are another way to uncover the missing pieces, the parts of us ready to 'come home' to integrate or be assimilated. I am cautious as I say this, for I do not believe all parts are meant to be integrated. Some are meant to go back down into the unconscious as we build the ego strength to refrain from literalizing fantasies or giving into the compulsion.

Nightmare themes may include dismemberment, murder, being chased, being hunted, and being haunted on some level. If the nightmare repeats, there is a lot of unexpressed energy there, and the soul is adamant about getting the message to us. Something wants to break into conscious awareness, but we may be pushing the entire thing down, not wanting to know, see, sense, or feel what it holds. This is another way we split ourselves apart, unconsciously separating our dream life from waking life, assuming the imagery and content of the dream is random or mental processing as the mind decompresses the day. Trust me, it is not what you ate or watched before bed, it is the psyche trying to speak to you. It will serve you well to listen; it just may be the message that helps you break free from the comfort of a psychological cage.

Many of my clients begin having chthonic symbols appear in their dreams, daydreams, and synchronistic moments. These are earth-based symbols. Our fear of the depths and our instinctual nature are reflected in our fear of death, evil, snakes, and all things close to the earth. All these elements have been used to control people; we see this in the rejection of the feminine in myth and religious retelling of stories. The serpent in the Garden of Eden is Satan tempting Eve with forbidden knowledge. It is a rite of passage to be swallowed by the night and merge with darkness, awakening power while interacting with the disorientating nature of chthonic symbols.

The snake shedding its skin is a transformative process—an unavoidable yet instinctual act. We have inherent aspects within us; the psyche is deeply intertwined with matter, cycles, seasons, and rhythms of nature. The snake as a symbol can inform us of potential ego interference and creative or destructive shadow elements. The serpent is a low-to-the-ground creature, a shadow form similar to the body, the feminine, the bowels, and the womb. Our instinctual nature brings us closer to earthly elements such as soil and bone. Attributes near the earth are feared and devalued; instead of honor, they carry projections of evil and fear.

> The serpent is a deeply feared chthonic animal, spiritually linked to awakening and transformation. Snakes hear through their skin and are sensitive to low-frequency vibrations. Many fear snakes because they are potent archetypal symbols of the unconscious. The snake is evidence of a profound transformation; it is both feared and respected as a reminder of our primal nature.

As we process unconscious material, the relationship to the symbol can change. We may begin seeing snakes in dreams and synchronistic moments. Somatically we may feel a subtle pull, a feeling to sit closer to the ground. Although it sounds ridiculous to the conscious mind, the psyche resonates with these concepts and continuously invokes them within. When we listen and pay attention to them, we are guided on how to gather our pieces, collecting the fragmented and broken parts of us left throughout our lives, which can lead to soul retrieval, psychic mending, and integration of lost parts.

The Fairy Tale: The Robber Bridegroom

A miller's daughter is engaged to a wealthy suitor. She didn't want to marry him. Although she has her father's approval, she feels uneasy about her future husband. She couldn't explain why—not in a way that made sense to her father, who saw only the suitor's money, fine clothes, and easy charm. She saw something else. Something in the way he looked at her. She felt it in her bones, and yet the engagement moved forward.

Then came the invitation. Her anxiety grows when he insists that she visit his home deep in the middle of the forest. "You must see my home," he told her. "Come to the woods. You'll love it there." The unease grew into something deeper. There was nothing for her in those woods—no neighbors, no friends, no witnesses. Her father insisted it was fine. "You're being silly. He's wealthy. He adores you."

She didn't argue, but she didn't go unprepared. Before she left, she filled her pockets with lentils and let them slip through her fingers as she walked, a quiet trail through the forest in case she needed to escape. The deeper she went, the worse she felt. Everything inside her said to stop, to turn back.

By the time she arrived, the sun was setting. The light was unusually red, bleeding light over the trees, deepening her uncertainty. His house—if you could call it that—stood in the clearing. It almost looked like an abandoned property, swallowed by the overgrowth of the forest. Secluded is an understatement. It was eerily quiet and deserted, but it wasn't empty.

An old woman stood at the door. She shouldn't have been there—this wasn't her house. When she saw the miller's daughter, her face lined with deep concern. She warns, "You shouldn't have come. You need to leave. Now." The maiden's stomach dropped; she didn't speak, just waited, and listened.

The anxiety grows in the miller's daughter as the old woman reveals that the house belongs to a band of robbers who intend to kill and eat her. "They'll be back soon," the old woman continued, glancing over her shoulder. "They don't bring you here to court you, girl. They bring you here to cut you up." And then—the sound.

Footsteps. Voices. Men. Terrified, the miller's daughter hides as the robbers return. The men are laughing and talking, as something lies on the ground between them. No, not something— someone. A girl, barely older than her, arms bound, mouth gagged, her body jerking violently in protest.

The miller's daughter feels her heart pound in her chest and her throat tighten as the robbers murder the woman. She sees the girl go still. And then the real horror began. She recoils in disgust and terror as they cut the body into pieces. Limb by limb, they tear her apart, reducing her to parts; dismembering her before eating her. The miller's daughter couldn't move, couldn't breathe, couldn't look away.

One of them picked up a hand and twisted it in the light, admiring something. A ring. He pried at it, but the slickness of the blood made it slip from his grip. The finger with the ring hit the floor and rolled straight toward the miller's daughter. She picks it up and tucks it into her pocket.

The men leave and the old woman comes back. "Now," the old woman whispered. "Run."

Through the trees. Through the dark. Through
the nightmare that refused to end. The lentils
were gone—eaten by birds. By the time she
reached home, she could barely speak. She fell
into her father's arms, sobbing, shaking, alive.

And the wedding? Oh, she kept the wedding.
Let him think she was still his quiet little bride-
to-be. Let him come. Let him stand before the
town, before witnesses, before the law. When
the time came, she raised her eyes to his and
declared, "I have a story to tell." She told them
everything. And when she was done, she opened
her hand and let the severed finger drop onto the
table. The gasps. The horror. They hanged him
and every one of his men before nightfall. The
miller's daughter never married. Some things,
once survived, make you impossible to claim.

Working the Fairy Tale

*What did you see, sense, or feel as
you read The Robber Bridegroom?*

Check in with your body, go to your darkness journal, and write down
any initial impressions, thoughts, or feelings.

Symbolism

How often do we dismiss or ignore the feeling in our belly that says,
"This doesn't feel right"? We do the thing anyway, wondering why we
didn't listen. Entering the dark forest is moving into the depths of the
unconscious. Just as she leaves a trail to find her way home, we can have
a talisman that reminds us of the way back to ourselves when we get lost.
We must always remember intuition is inherent within, an inner compass
we should trust over all other tools for navigation. Our intuition can
show us where we need mending and re-membering.

We can instinctively begin to detect the parts of us that intend to destroy
and cannibalize. These parts seek to consume our innocence and devour
our goodness. Witnessing the murder can be the way we split ourselves
into pieces, creating distance from what we don't want to see, sense, or
feel; enabling our destructive, chaotic, and unhealthy coping mechanisms
versus learning to be with the shadow element that is presenting itself.
Some things are easier to break down when pulled apart into smaller
pieces and dismembered to make our consumption more convenient.

The finger falls to the ground. The finger is one small part that tells the whole truth of the story. This finger has a ring; this circular object is associated with wholeness—a symbol of completion, coming full circle, the end of an ordeal. There is always one part of us that can 'point' to a pattern, revealing the larger story or myth at hand. When the essential parts have been reclaimed (fingers), we can re-member wholeness through the lens of duality. Darkness is sometimes the primordial space where birth or deconstruction occurs, wiping the slate clean to create a new beginning and mending the soul.

Your Turn: Dismembered

Limb by limb, sometimes we are taken apart to be put back together again. Sometimes, the shadow is a sword cutting into the heart of the matter. It needs to be dissecting, dismembering, uncomfortable, and ugly. Although this sounds horrendous, and it can be, it is purposeful and comes with the possibility that once you come together again, you will have a sense of renewal like never before, a trust that is unshakable, a soul that knows the depths and can no longer go back to living on the surface of things.

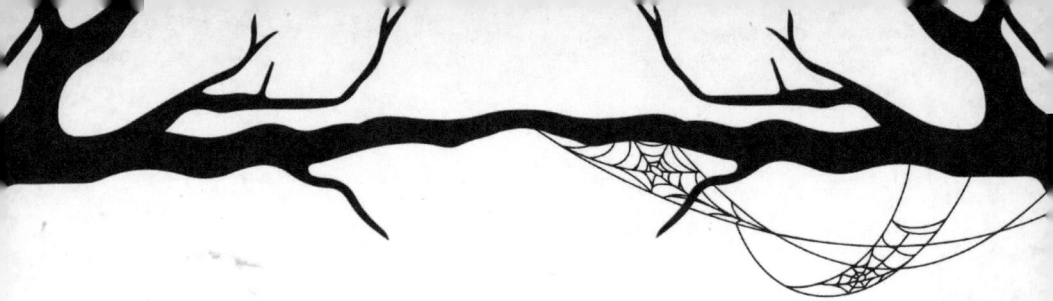

Journal Prompts

What tears you apart or tries to separate you from your knowing?

How do you ignore your feelings or insights to make others happy? Has this ever caused you harm?

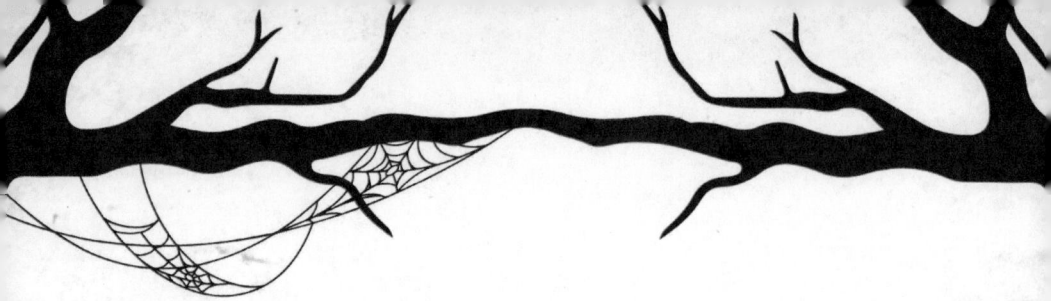

Is there a part of you that feels cut off or separate from the rest?

What needs to be "re-membered" or brought back together again?

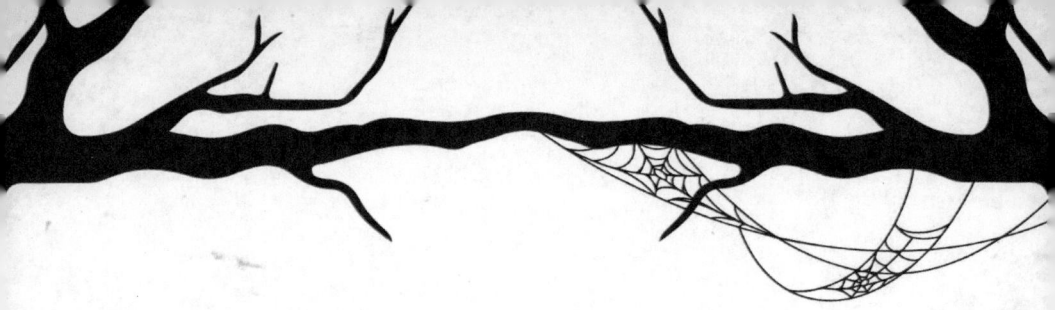

Sit with a circumstance of severance, free write on it in your darkness journal, and see what wisdom wants to come out of the wound.

Reflection

This chapter reflected on the motif of
psychological dismemberment as a necessary
part of transformation. We often become
fragmented, and yet it is in this breaking
apart that the opportunity for psychic
mending occurs. By acknowledging what
has been severed within, we begin the
sacred work of re-membering ourselves—
piece by piece—into a state of wholeness.
Reflect on being in pieces, what pieces have
your attention now? Write about it...

08

CHAPTER

Poisoned

She Who Consumes Darkness

Poison comes in many forms. It can hide in the devouring madness of an addiction or blend into the subtle sound of your voice as it nags and berates you inside your head. Poison may be hidden in the warm embrace of an enemy or disguised as love from a jealous parent. Poison can be what and how we consume. Poison teaches us where we lose ourselves when consumed by the presence of another's needs. We can transmute the poison we hold for ourselves and others. Once poison is understood, it can become an unexpected ally. It teaches us the power of holding the tension instead of escaping the pressure.

We must be careful of growing appetites, for there are numerous parallels between addiction and highly sensitive individuals; both are susceptible to getting lost in an experience or being consumed by a substance, an idea, or another's influence. Being highly sensitive is a gift, yet it means we need stronger boundaries since we tend to magnetize the poisonous nature of another, especially the things others are unconscious of. A shared vulnerability exists among the sensitive and the addicted. Many struggle to be in this world, and some are extremely sensitive and highly empathic; their porous nature may add a soulful dimension to their work, life, and creativity, though sometimes this comes at a cost to their well-being.

The sensitive or addicted one will be brought to the underworld, the underbelly of experiences. The poisons of the underworld are limitless, and we may be dragged unwillingly by a relentless idea or compulsion we cannot shake. It is not bad; it is not a punishment; we must not get this twisted with hell or other religious associations. It is the mythological dynamic of the psyche at work within us, part of the self-regulation of the psyche to help us transmute and transform.

Our devouring nature and patterns of consumption are contained within the shadow. Compulsions are the parts of us operating unconsciously, caught in relentless cycles perpetuated by core wounds. Cyclical in nature, patterns governed by a compulsion are driven by hidden agendas. Shadow work requires us to face these elements to see what has been repressed, rejected, or abandoned. We can learn to channel these elements, integrating them once certain aspects have been transmuted. Before we can transform shadow aspects, it helps to discuss transmutation a bit further.

Transmutation is an alchemical process. It often occurs beneath awareness, a symptom of change that is sometimes invisible to the naked eye. We may transmute suffering, darkness, and shadow material into another form such as consciousness, power, or understanding. By confronting our darkness, we diminish its power while strengthening our resolve and fortifying our connection to the authentic self. When we block the transmutation process by denying or suppressing it, it can become poisonous. The emotion, feeling, sensation, and information does not go away; it eventually descends back into the unconscious.

To transmute shadow material, we need to investigate it. To do so is an invitation to engage with the material creatively. We might give a difficult feeling, sensation, or circumstance a symbol to better understand the energy that is trying to move into consciousness. Common symbols of transmutation are the alembic vessel in alchemy (the glass that holds the ingredients to allow the change to occur), the ouroboros (serpent or dragon devouring its tail), or the phoenix (rising from the ashes). These symbols help one intuitively work with shadow material in a creative way. We must become students again if we wish to transmute energy, which asks us to learn how to see, sense, and feel with curiosity. We learn to see not only with the eyes but with the psyche and to trust the psyche to guide us as we transmute poison into medicine or nectar.

We can learn to engage with the poisons intentionally, noticing psychological patterns and bodily sensations. What we see and how it sees us tells us about our psyche and consciousness. We can intuitively enter the dark spaces of the mind and body and excavate enormous power and potential. We can learn to respect darkness, depth, and death—necessary archetypal processes in life. We must confront our pathological states and normalized cultural dysfunctions and begin tending to the wounds that perpetuate our desire to escape or destroy ourselves, becoming conscious of what we take in physically and emotionally and aware of the cost of our appetites.

As we examine our appetites, we may have to examine what nourishes and what poisons us. Poison is the thing that undoes us, yet in the undoing, something else is born. A poison may be necessary for us to contend with, especially while exploring the shadow as a part of the individuation process. We become poisoned by what we hold, and when we become accustomed to poison, we are addicted to it. This includes helping and supporting others while abandoning our own needs. It need not be an addiction to a substance, but a behavior that creates a power dynamic. A situation where we unconsciously give power away repeatedly to feel the rush of being needed or loved. As we work with the shadow, staying tethered to the present moment is vital. This keeps us from escaping or giving in to the desire to merge with something more significant in a state of oceanic bliss while avoiding pain. Without a sense of self or an anchor, we may spiral further into the spaces we try to outrun.

> I have had countless ego deaths and dark nights of the soul woven with mystery, along with the desire to dissociate, get lost in the nostalgia of childhood, struggle with current reality, and release the grip of self-destruction and addiction through awakening consciousness.

There was a time when I could not access the universe's magic without substances, falsely creating a sense of enchantment. An inner battle ensued when my ego and soul were in opposition, a deep longing and inner void that could never be filled without a hint of drama or chaos.

Some of us intentionally swallow poison, indulging and disappearing into altered states to access creativity or connection, while others find themselves bewildered by the disorientating nature of the unconscious. Poison or potential: we encounter both as we interact with the unconscious. There is a fine line between holding and transmuting darkness and allowing it to consume us. We may chew on an idea, toying with creative tension as it builds and generates energy. Once we answer the call, we are pulled into the depths. We may be captivated or seduced by the allure of an idea—there are temptations and pitfalls of poisons for an individual in touch with their depth.

Just as the mind is multifaceted and complex with intangible qualities, compulsions are systems within a hidden structure contained within the shadow. We can look to the shadow to discover all that is constellated within: untapped potential, drives, desires, and ways one navigates life based on their complexes.

As we transmute the old, we sometimes need to revisit specific processes. Spiraling is a movement of individuation; as we revisit an aspect of the process, we mature and become more refined in our unfolding. This can result in an understanding of instincts and deeper impulses. The process happens as needed in its timing and sometimes repetitively.

I have continuously been drawn to the shadow side of my sensitivity, intrigued by the edgy, dark, and intense energies that evoke and stir through certain films and forensic cases. These qualities have acclimated me to better understand the collective shadow. This part of the psyche contains hidden, repulsive, chaotic, and sometimes what may be described as evil elements we find difficult to face within ourselves or the world as a collective. Many of us are doing powerful work to transmute and transform the shadow in intense yet creative ways.

An example is how Evan Peters chose to portray the serial killer Jeffery Dahmer in a highly controversial role in the series *Monster: The Jeffrey Dahmer Story*. The experience challenged Peters. He publicly commented on how it took him into dark places as he confronted the psychology of intense human behavior by studying Dahmer so intently, becoming him on some level to better emulate him. Everything I read about Peters made me wonder how actors help us understand and assimilate darkness by presenting taboo characters.

Peters' portrayal of Dahmer reminded me of the story of the Hindu deity Shiva. Peters was changed by this experience, to what degree even he may never know. I had a vision of Peters with a blue throat becoming Dahmer, as if the actor's psyche was grappling with how much of this energy to swallow. I believe this role collectively transmuted aspects hidden within the shadow of the United States culture at the time. Shiva is often depicted with a blue throat or blue skin to represent the process of transmutation. Transmutation, like any other process, requires a space and period of liminality, an in-between state. Shiva depicts this with his blue throat; he draws in all the poison (darkness, shadow, evil elements) and holds them in his throat, eventually turning him blue. Shiva does this to combat the darkness of the world. In his throat, the poison sits and moves through transmutation, a change from toxic poison to the sweetness of nectar.

Peters gave us a lens into Dahmer's psyche from a distance. This example shows us how art serves us and creatively assimilates shadow material.

To illustrate this physically, we can learn the art of transmutation by observing a bruise. Just as a bruise changes color as it heals, reminding us of physical recovery, shadow work offers a significant psychological transformation taking place within. Shiva, as an archetypal symbol, shows us poison is safe to consume in manageable amounts and, in the correct dose, can even be the medicine. For some, this is the work we have done from a young age.

Understanding our core wounding, the impactful moments, and traumas we experience early on allows us to see the places that are tender and unconsciously pulling us into situations to gain further clarity on our blind spots. Chiron, mythologically, is known as the wounded healer, an archetypal energy known to reveal the part of us that never heals and becomes the medicine we offer to the world. This is how darkness changes from the poison to the nectar, the burden becomes a gift. Before we accept our gifts, they may overpower us and create chaos in our lives.

Sometimes I would unknowingly expose something that wasn't meant to be shared, not because I was trying to be hurtful or tell a secret; I had a gift that involved exposing and transmuting shadow. It took years to unwind the belief that I was a tattletale or bad friend. I didn't understand the nature of secrets. I could not fathom holding onto something painful instead of transmuting the energy and lifting the burden from the heart.

Now, I know why I have a gift of holding darkness. It is not to amplify or glorify it; it is to help others unburden their hearts. Shadow work expands our capacity to hold opposing experiences without abandoning ourselves, working with difficult, even taboo topics to bring unconscious elements forward. In this view, we may see the shadow worker as an alchemist, transforming pain into wisdom.

Many of us are unlearning the programming that creates shame and guilt for our deeply feeling and sensitive nature. We need to stop apologizing for knowing things before they happen and apologizing for our magnetism toward all that is hidden. We can dialogue with this unique aspect of self, which is drawn to hold the darkness for others. One can discover sacred meaning by channeling darkness and shadow into a creative expression or form.

Perhaps you carry darkness for others. I wish someone had told me sooner that there was a potent and transformative aspect to this pattern, that those of us who carry shadow for others hold unconscious patterns in service of transformation. Before it was a gift, it manifested as a curse. This is easier to see as we explore the archetypal energetics of the scapegoat and black sheep. The archetypal shadow carriers are the scapegoat and the black sheep; both hold an immensely immeasurable burden with a potent destiny to fulfill. These roles are projected upon an individual who does not know they contain a latent transformative power. When we choose to stay the course and hold the tension, illusions may fall away, emotions and somatic experiences might surface, and we can become attuned to our dark side in a healthy way. Shadow work changes us, and people notice those changes. As we confront our own shadows, those who observe our changes find themselves significantly impacted and sometimes triggered, for better or worse.

Change can activate abandonment and rejection wounds. What we see unfolding may trigger the ego, and it will want to cling to the old familiar ways we knew someone or something to be. It stings to be on either side of this dynamic. It is common for backlash, drama, and negative feedback to emerge as you dive deeper and deeper into the true self. People will want to hold onto the version of you they have grown to know and love, regardless of how much pain and suffering that old version held.

Rituals are a critical part of transmuting darkness. Rituals have helped me through dark nights and intense periods of change. Rituals became tools to transform addictive patterns and to move through difficult times. The shadow sometimes expresses in an impulsive moment, a desire to run away or create something new. Inspirations can be magnetic yet also disruptive. When not balanced, they lead to radical moves that result in chaos and confusion, igniting a rebellious force of energy. We can be misled by the desire to liberate ourselves from the monotony of life.

Rituals can move us in and out of various psychological states. It is important to be mindful of how to return from the underworld and integrate the lessons and experiences from the process. Rituals help us come home to who we are; they are a passage out of the underworld.

It can be too easy to lose oneself in the things we devour and consume. After symbolically transmuting the poison, we can return with an offering, such as the hero returning with the medicine to offer to his or her community.

The symbolic return denotes the integration of the potions and poisons from the process. A ritual can help one awaken wisdom through somatic practices such as a hot salt bath, changing place or location, or another gesture that declares completion. Hopefully, the process has left its mark regardless of the outcome. My medicine woman led me through a profound journey, and one day, she reminded me to look for the journey's markings, to see these milestones, moments, and obstacles as the energetic scars that shape us. These energetic scars are also known as samskaras. Samskara is a Sanskrit name denoting an archetypal or psychological imprint. The moments and memories of the encounters stay with us.

The Fairy Tale: Snow White

A beautiful young princess becomes the target of her jealous stepmother, the Queen. Snow White knew her stepmother watched her. There was something in the way the woman's eyes lingered a second too long, something too sharp in her smiles. She wasn't cruel at first—not openly—but her love was a weapon, wielded with precision, suffocating, and full of something sickly sweet.

The Queen has a magical mirror she regularly consults, asking, "Who is the fairest of them all?" For years, the mirror assures her that she is the fairest. Then, one day, the answer changed. The mirror shockingly declares Snow White is the fairest of them all. The Queen's once doting attention turned cold. Consumed by rage and jealousy, the Queen orders a huntsman to take Snow White into the forest and kill her.

The huntsman came for her in the morning. He didn't say much, just that they were going for a walk. She wasn't stupid. She saw how his hands shook and the way he avoided eye contact. But she followed.

They walked deep into the woods, where the trees consumed the sunlight, where no one could hear you scream. Then, he turned to her, voice raw, eyes desperate. "Run." That was all he said.

The huntsman could not bring himself to harm Snow White so he let her go.

She ran. She didn't look back. Didn't ask questions. Didn't stop. She ran until her legs gave out and her lungs burned. And when she opened her eyes, she saw it—a small cabin hidden in the trees. The cabin was a mess, but it was shelter.

Snow White spent the next few days making it livable—clearing the dust, scrubbing the grime, making the bed as if this were a temporary inconvenience. Then they came. Seven dwarves— grimy, rough, hardened by years of labor, their hands thick with calluses, their eyes cold with something she couldn't quite name. They let her stay—for a price.

At first, she happily lived with them, keeping house, tending to their wounds, and cooking while they worked the mines. She did what was necessary. The dwarves left every morning and she stayed behind, trapped in a house that felt less like a refuge and more like a prison. She told herself this was survival. Then the Queen found her. The mirror informed the Queen that Snow White was still alive. She devised a plan to fool Snow White.

Snow White opened the door the first time because the woman seemed harmless—just an old peddler with kind eyes and a gentle voice. But the moment she let her in, the hands came fast—yanking the bodice tight, crushing her ribs, squeezing the air from her lungs. She collapsed. The dwarves found her hours later, unconscious on the floor, barely breathing. They cut the laces and let the air rush back into her lungs. She woke up gasping.

The second time, she knew better. But the old woman was different—softer, kinder, desperate to help. She didn't see the hands move until it was too late—until the poisoned comb was buried in her hair, pressing deep into her scalp. She dropped without a sound. The dwarves found her again and pulled the comb out.

The third time, it was the poisoned apple. And this time, they didn't find her in time. Snow White didn't remember much after the apple. Just the world fading, the dwarves' voices calling her name, a strange feeling of weightlessness as if the earth had fallen away beneath her. She didn't die. Not completely. But she couldn't move, couldn't scream, couldn't fight. Snow White had fallen into a death-like sleep. The dwarves laid her in a glass coffin, assuming she is dead. Days passed. Weeks. The dwarves stopped talking about her. The house was quieter. Then, he came—the prince.

He was fascinated with her lying still in the glass coffin. He wouldn't stop looking, wouldn't stop touching. "She's beautiful," he murmured. The dwarves told him she was dead. He didn't care. He wanted her. He leans in and kisses her, breaking the spell. Snow White gasps, startled as she awakens from her slumber. Snow White and the prince eventually marry.

The Queen never stood a chance. From the moment she arrived at the wedding Snow White watched her and waited. The stepmother's face went pale when she saw her, realizing too late that Snow White wasn't buried after all. Snow White didn't forgive. They locked the Queen in a room with a pair of iron shoes, glowing red-hot from the fire. "Dance," they told her. And she did.

Until her feet blackened and peeled. Until she collapsed from the pain. Until the life drained from her eyes, and she finally stopped moving. Snow White had learned that poison isn't always in the apple; it's in words, in hands that pretend to be kind, in love that corrodes from the inside. Not all poisons kill instantly; some seep in slowly, softening you until you break without knowing why. The trick to survival wasn't just avoiding poison. It was learning to recognize it, taste it before swallowing, and, when necessary, know how to use it yourself.

What did you see, sense, or feel as you read Snow White?

Check in with your body, go to your darkness journal, and write down any initial impressions, thoughts, or feelings.

Symbolism

Anger and jealousy consume us, as do the stories we tell ourselves. We may obsess over what we see or don't see appearing in the mirror. Perfectionism and narcissism poison the self by inflating the ego and amplifying the persona. We see all this as the Queen holds up her trusty mirror, expecting it to adore her. There are moments when we cannot fight the compulsion, the need that arises as the ego requires a hit of superiority. The huntsman is asked to kill this perceived threat yet fails to comply. In a battle between an innocent target (Snow White) and a predator (huntsman), for the moment, innocence wins.

We must look at the poisons we ingest as we develop and mature; many unconsciously crave love or acceptance from a parental figure. If the parents are absorbed in themselves, they will only see their reflection, with no room for the child to have one of their own. The child suffers and may feel invisible. Growing up, we turn into adults who consume and believe ugly ideas about ourselves, our presence, and our bodies.

These psychological poisons are crippling and become unconscious patterns, leading to a variety of afflictions or addictions. We start unconsciously poisoning ourselves, consuming substances to unknowingly seek to reconnect with the remnants of our distorted versions of mother or father. The altered state is created from the substance fabricated to replicate the state from adolescence. We may gravitate to a poison as a surrogate for our devouring parent. The potion becomes the act of noticing where we go unconscious and fall into a trance. We may notice when we abandon ourselves. We may notice who is put before others. We may notice ourselves generally and the reflections we craved but never received. It can be painful to look this closely.

We may look to the dwarves as helpers, parts of the psyche guiding and supporting Snow White in the process of individuation—various qualities and parts that come together to move her forward. The dwarves are like separate parts that need to be integrated, fragmented aspects of the soul, the splintering within, and the separation of feeling and intuition from the body. She must first fall into a death-like sleep (altered state of consciousness) for the integration to occur.

Snow White had three attempts to kill her, a reminder that our intuition can only reach us when we choose to listen. If we are driven by compulsion, blind to our unmet needs, or overwhelmed by the darkness of another, we are more vulnerable to the poison.

Sometimes, we have done nothing wrong, yet we will be targeted anyway. If we return to the deeper impulse of the self, one can find the remedy, the potion. There are countless ways to read the tale. Each time we explore the narrative, we invite a different insight into our conscious awareness.

To transmute poison into potential, one must be willing to take a hard look at patterns of consumption—how we devour and unconsciously swallow what we are fed; how we take in darkness; and who and what the sources are. The emotional wound that never closes, the infection that burrows deeper—these reveal how we poison ourselves through enabling patterns we refuse to see. When poisoned, we may need to step back, flush the system, and closely evaluate who and what is making us sick. Some need to hold the poison longer, while others have waited too long. Only you know the right dose for you.

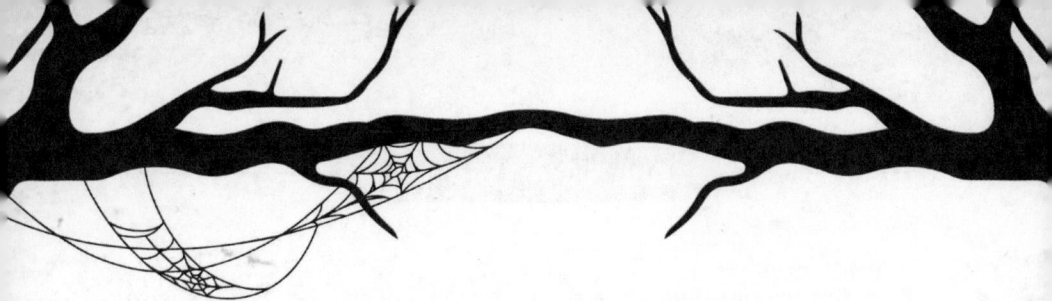

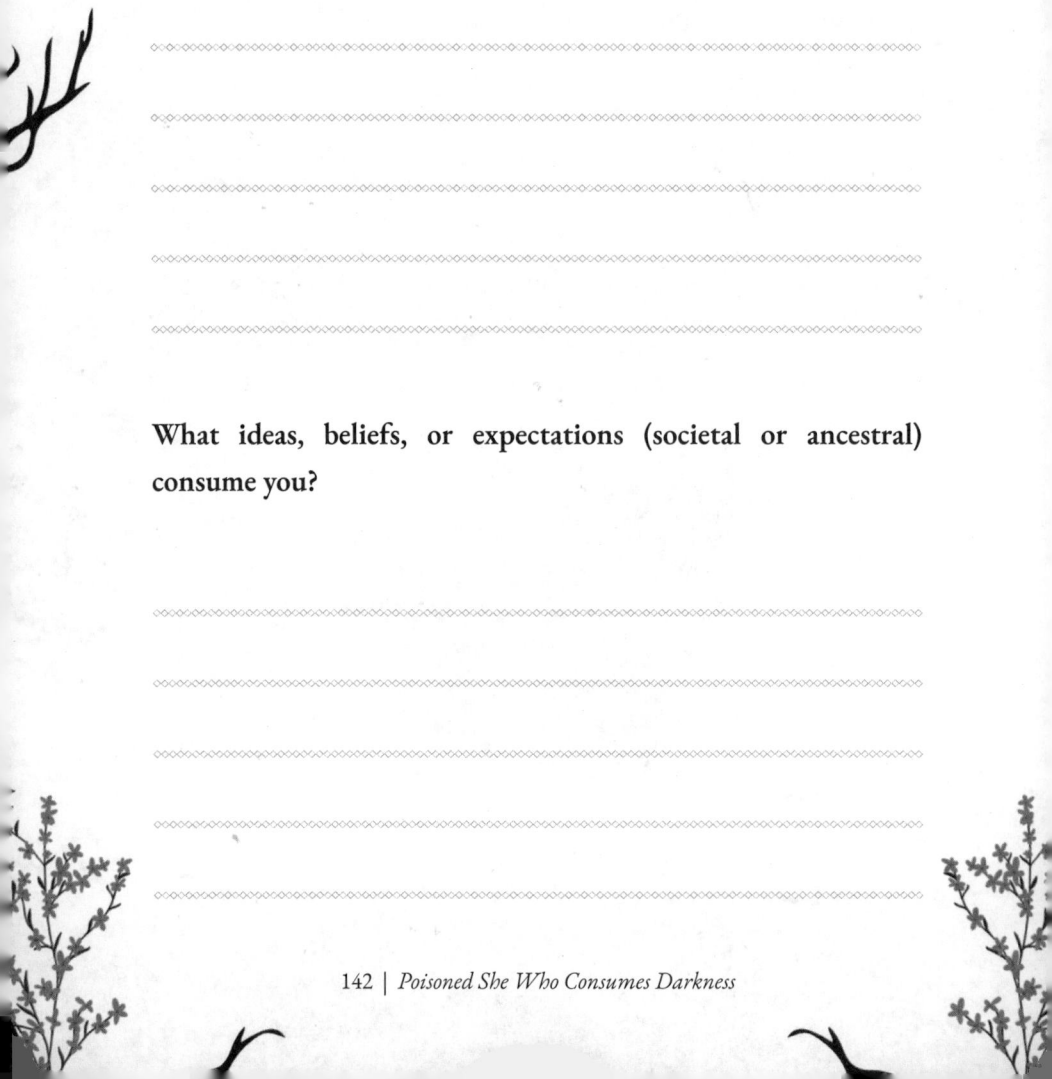

Journal Prompts

What 'good thing' becomes poisonous when you have too much?

What ideas, beliefs, or expectations (societal or ancestral) consume you?

Can you trace a repetitive wound, the vicious circling of energy that never seems to cease?

Name your poison, free write on it in your darkness journal, and see what wisdom wants to come out of the wound.

Reflection

This chapter invited us to consider
the poisons we consume emotionally,
psychologically, and spiritually, and how
they affect us. In *Snow White*, we saw how
poison can come in the form of envy, unmet
needs, or internalized narratives, and how
recognizing this is the first step toward
transmuting it into power. To become whole,
we must discern the poisons we swallow
and transform them through awareness and
ritual; the medicine is often hidden in the
wound. How does this idea land within? Let
it fester and channel it out onto the page...

06
CHAPTER

Numb

She Who
Is Frozen

Numbness is a trickster, changing from one form to another. Numbness and being frozen are doorways into the shadow. Initially, we may view being frozen or numb as a lack of feeling with little to no sensation, movement, or presence of emotion. Numbness is sneaky as it distracts us. We are convinced something does not exist because we lack evidence of the typical symptoms or sensations that make us uncomfortable.

For this reason, freezing and numbness are rich with hidden power, openings into what first appears as a dead zone. There are multiple symptoms of freezing and numbness, physical and emotional. Both indicate where we feel burdened, stuck, or unable to move. Those gifted at holding the darkest parts of other people's psyches and stories are vulnerable to freezing, numbness, and compassion fatigue. Media has us buying into limitless ways we can anesthetize ourselves. We are lulled back to sleep and placed in a trance as we dismiss the soul's attempts to awaken feeling, sensation, and power.

One can be frozen in time and body. My work revolves around psychologically and metaphorically gathering and retrieving the parts of the self that have been scattered throughout time due to impactful moments. Some aspects of us are frozen in time (referred to as arrested development) when part of us splinters off at a specific age due to an impactful or traumatic moment. To be frozen could indicate we lack the capacity or resources to take action. Like a psychic winter, everything slows down. Being in a frozen state is not weakness but an attempt by the psyche to protect itself from what it is not yet ready to face.

As a coping mechanism, we may regress to the age or emotional state of an originating incident. Being unable to successfully accommodate the unmet need at the time is like being under a spell or in a trance, except we are frozen in time. This is a trance of disempowerment where the psyche cannot move us toward wholeness, and we struggle to advance, grow, or heal.

Shadow work helps us metaphorically break unconscious spells, the trance that affirms we are not good enough. As we return to consciousness, we break the trance and thaw out. It is important to consider that the self-regulating aspect of the psyche may require us to go into the unconscious to reveal blind spots, uncovering ways we are disenchanted and perhaps influenced by a variety of sources and unaware of it. This ties back to the shamanic perspective of soul loss, which we explored earlier. These patterns are also a form of cognitive dissonance, occurring when various parts of us conflict. There may be a sense of incongruence when we encounter these disparate parts. Shadow work is best done creatively so the ego softens its defenses. This is another reason for using creative and intense forms such as film, fairy tales, and forensics to address psychic fragmentation.

We may abandon the body and become numb to certain areas while plagued by density, a gravitational pull trying to keep us tethered to the earth, creating a sense of being trapped. Like a groove from water moving through a cavern, the grooves deepen and collect debris beneath the moving water over time. Negative thoughts anchor the mind like the debris trapped beneath a moving current. Wounding creates defensive armoring to create distance from the thoughts, feelings, and memories, but it blocks the mystery of life and enchantment. What begins as a psychic defense of a protective nature to combat painful experiences eventually establishes unhealthy patterns and armor. Early traumatic events led to denial, projection, introjection, and splitting, resulting in a desire to numb when life became too much, a splitting off from bodily awareness reflecting the intensity of an impactful experience. Knowing how to care for oneself is unfortunately not always modeled. We might default to substances as synthetic comfort. We can feel hypervigilant and attentive to the needs of others when in their presence.

As a deeply intuitive child, I believed my voice didn't matter, so I compensated with coping mechanisms such as people-pleasing. I kept my inner world to myself and experienced crippling anxiety in school, inhibiting my ability to speak in front of others. Bullying affirmed that I couldn't trust others, yet it was the bullies inside my family tree that hurt more than those passing in the school hallways. I did not yet have the language or understanding of what it meant to internalize my emotions and thoughts. I would physically feel my body freeze with any attention from my peers, teachers, and most of my family.

Growing up, the world around me affirmed it wasn't safe to feel deeply; otherwise, we carry the dreadful badge of the sensitive ones. In my mind, this translated to weak and fragile. Then, I discovered the concept of the glass child, which immediately validated my experience. I felt at home the more research I did on it. Before then, I had never felt seen, yet everything changed when I learned about the psychological phenomenon of the glass child and oriented my shadow work around this aspect of myself and my clients.

The glass child is afflicted by an internal conflict that vacillates between the comfortable safety of being invisible and a relentless hunger to be seen. The glass child was raised in an environment that commanded attention and care to be given to someone other than them. This may have been a sibling or parent with some type of physical, emotional, or psychological need that superseded their own, a level of care that pulled attention away from them to give to the vulnerable sibling or parent. Another aspect could have been a narcissistic or neglectful parent(s) who was unable to mirror the child and validate their existence.

A common association of the glass child is invisibility, which is carried as a deep wound and can create situations for the child to turn into an adult who never receives credit for their hard work, who only gives support and never receives it, who sees others and has a massive heart—yet never feels seen or reciprocated.

The glass child has developed strength by relying on themselves. They are highly self-sufficient, can be untrusting of others, and relate more closely to animals and the natural world. The glass child is never seen, always overlooked, and rarely is given the attention they seek. They learn to fulfill their own needs, becoming a loner and highly independent. Often, they become a dependable form of support for others to the degree that they are taken advantage of. They become invisible, blending into the background until needed, then forgotten again.

We can also see the glass child as being suspended in time, frozen or numb. Like glass, ice has parallel qualities, and numbing behavior is central to this archetypal pattern. These individuals become acclimated with a sadness that encapsulates them, helping to insulate them from the loneliness they feel from holding so much for others. They internalize pain, learn to soften their voice (if it isn't stolen from them), and struggle with a sense of value or self-worth. The glass child is vulnerable on the inside, so they shatter and fragment easily. They may ice people out, give them the cold shoulder, or isolate.

Paradoxically, these individuals are incredibly strong outwardly, yet the continued failure of needs never being met and expressions never being honored wears them down, and they collapse within themselves. Anger, rage, shame, and guilt are difficult to express. They internalize these emotions since they must be strong for others. Anger is sometimes the courage of sadness. The word anger is rooted in "affliction" and means to be tied together.

Symbolically we might imagine ice: it can be hard and solidified, yet also extremely delicate and vulnerable. Ice can also symbolize a paralyzed psyche—someone caught in a liminal state, emotions frozen, a heart that has gone cold. When we are frozen, we may not have access to other parts of the psyche or shadow, signaling an emotional disconnect. Yet the beauty of the shadow is all can be retrieved, and in this case, thaw and return to life.

As the glass child awakens, they start to heal. They warm themselves by offering themselves the attention, love, and care others could not give them. They start assimilating and integrating the lost pieces of the psyche, mending them through patience and learning to hold space for themselves. This often occurs before it is observed in the outer world around them. In relationships, it takes time for them to feel safe and contained as boundaries are initially difficult, and they are learning to hold energy and power instead of giving it away or having it siphoned by others. The glass child must create an identity and self-validate as they heal the energetic complexes that keep them in the vicious cycle of numbing or disappearing; they must learn to hold themselves physically, emotionally, and psychologically.

Not all mothering is created equal. If we lack the presence of powerful and healthy feminine influences in childhood, we may lack the modeling of a healthy container psychologically or emotionally for nurturing. Some of us are learning how to feel safe and be held in new ways: spiritually, physically, and psychologically. The archetypal nature of the orphan overlaps with the glass child through an amplified pattern of abandonment or rejection. The idea of 'not belonging' can ignite an ego defense, as the ego seeks to protect us during that experience. The glass child must do the inner work and examine the part of herself that sabotages her intentions by remaining small, hidden, and invisible as she carries the burden of another (as a good scapegoat does). She must confront how she hides her pain and masks her quirks to fit into the places she never belonged.

To awaken what is numb, she may enter a wound to collect the broken parts of self and create new forms from the damaged and scattered fragments of a broken image, a reclamation and declaration of the authentic self that was not permitted to exist before. We innately know how to heal—the body knows. This aspect of shadow work engages the body as a vital part of healing process. I created a process called Somatic Detection™; think of it as learning how to decode the psychology of the body through feeling and sensation. Somatic techniques are essential for moving our awareness toward something called the psychoid, the part of the psyche that is linked to the body (soma). Somatic practices are mindful movements, such as yoga, that take time to be with sensations as they rise and fall. Another example is walking with awareness of how the entire foot touches the earth, how the muscles move, and how we locate our physical bodies within the space we occupy.

Somatic techniques are body-centered approaches to healing that integrate the mind, emotions, and physical sensations. There are two core tenets to somatic work that apply to assimilating shadow material: titration and pendulation. Titration involves processing small amounts of trauma instead of confronting it as a whole, breaking it down so it is manageable for the nervous system. Pendulation is a way of alternating between tension and relaxation to release stored energy or emotions in a slow and intentional way.

As deeply feeling or sensitive souls, somatic-based practices facilitate containment, the holding of an experience. This can reorient us to deadened, unexplored, or forgotten spaces within the body. Somatic experiences activate an innate inner intelligence; it is a duty and a blessing to tend to the soul through the inclusivity of the body, embodying dark and abandoned locales.

Somatic techniques allow integration to take on a lasting quality, bringing it into the bones to make it real. To be physically or psychologically held in a safe and supportive manner permits us to explore body sensations and repattern thoughts, feelings, and beliefs about what it means to be nurtured. Some of us only feel safe holding darkness for others, shutting parts of us out, especially when mothering (or the energy of nurturing) has been unsafe. Mothers are not always kind and loving. A devouring mother can be dismissive rather than loving and kind, a shadow revealing patterns of narcissism and other disturbing personality characteristics.

At a young age, sensitives observe emotion and quickly detect manipulation, affirming it is not safe to be kind, soft, and empathetic. We unconsciously began armoring—food, substances, or anything to dampen our sensitive nature like a deer living among wolves. We apologize for who we are and carry guilt for simply being. Walls go up within and around us. Boundaries are not always easy; cultivating them can be messy. The longer we live with certain constructs of how we should be or what is appropriate engagement with others, the more our boundaries can become walls, creating division and separation.

Somatically, we can shift the archetypal energy of a mother from a devouring witch to a nurturing essence. When stored emotions are released, the body releases density and is free to hold power. Understanding the heavy, dense, constricted, and numb aspects of the body unlocks the symbolic meaning of sensation, and unconscious patterns are replaced by conscious expressions of a unified whole.

A shadow aspect of numbness is the overwhelming pain one may feel as an awakening begins. Sensation, feeling, and intuition are heightened as our life force permeates frozen tissue and psychological terrain. What appears to be dead, dark, or necrotic contains the most invisible light and comes to life with a force that can first appear unsettling. We unconsciously pass along pain. The body contains unspoken words; sometimes, we silence our feelings if our efforts to express them are stifled. The body begins to act like a suitcase dragging behind us. Pulling on invisible threads, we wait and follow to see what is next to unravel. All that was stifled may begin to awaken with a force that frightens us or others.

The Fairy Tale: Sleeping Beauty

The birth of the princess was a joyous and prosperous time. The king and queen host a grand celebration to honor the arrival of their new baby. They invited everyone who mattered—nobles, royals, the highest-ranking clergy. The banquet tables were piled high with food, the wine flowed endlessly, and the gold-trimmed invitations were delivered to every fairy in the kingdom.

Except one. All but one fairy is invited to bless the child. Fairy number thirteen was considered unlucky and was not welcome. No one spoke of her, but everyone knew why. She was bitter, old, strange; the kind of woman who made people uncomfortable; the kind they gossiped about.

So, they left her off the guest list. But she came anyway.

She arrived at the celebration draped in black, her face unreadable. The fairy is angry for how she has been treated. And when the king's guards moved to stop her, she simply lifted a single finger. The room went silent and cold. Then she spoke.

"She will bleed. And she will die." A curse, simple and brutal. On her sixteenth birthday, the princess will prick her finger on a spinning wheel and die a horrible death. The queen lets out a scream. The king—pale, furious, helpless— looked to the other fairies, begging for a way out.

Another fairy would not have it. "She won't die," the good fairy stammered. "She'll only sleep. For a hundred years. Until someone wakes her." The only way the princess can awaken is to be kissed by a prince.

The king ordered every spinning wheel in the kingdom destroyed. Doing their best to protect their daughter, they forbid all spinning wheels from the kingdom. Everyone watched the flames consume the spinning wheels piled high in the courtyard. But you can't erase something just because you don't want to see it.

There was still one spinning wheel left forgotten in a closet, in an obscure part of the castle. And on her sixteenth birthday, the princess found it. Nobody knows how she got there. They had swathed her in protection, walled her off from the world, cocooned her in safety so tightly that she had never questioned what lay beyond. She had never seen a spinning wheel, touched one, or even known what she was meant to fear. And yet, as she moved through the corridors of the castle on the morning of her sixteenth birthday, something inside her stirred, pulled, reached.

The princess finds the spinning wheel. Her hand lifts before she understands why. Her finger meets the spindle and pierces it. She collapses, falling into a deep sleep. They tried everything. Doctors, spells, prayers. But she didn't wake up. She was breathing. She was warm. But she was gone.

The king couldn't stand it and sealed the castle. The servants, the guards, the courtiers were all put into a deep sleep by the good fairy. Years passed. Then decades. Then a century. The kingdom outside the castle forgot. They stopped telling the story. Stopped believing she had ever been real.

But the castle was still there, hidden from the world by a thick forest. Still languishing in the dark, the walls heavy with vines, the bodies trapped inside untouched, frozen in time. Until one hundred years later, a prince hears of the legend of the sleeping princess. The prince came.

He ventures through the dense forest, cutting his way through the overgrowth and chopping through the vines. And then he found her. She was still there, the princess, exactly as she had been the day she went to sleep. No decay. No rot. As if time itself had stopped around her. Her skin was still pale, her lips still soft, her chest still rising and falling with slow, unnatural breaths.

She didn't move.

He knew what the story said, so he kissed her. Something exhaled. Not the princess. The castle. The walls trembled. The vines retreated. The bodies stirred. She sat up slowly. Her eyes opened and she smiled. The servants woke up. The guards. The courtiers. They blinked, turned their heads, and looked at the prince like they had never seen a human before. Because they hadn't. Not for a long, long time. The curse had broken.

*What did you see, sense, or feel
as you read Sleeping Beauty?*

Check in with your body, go to your darkness journal, and write down
any initial impressions, thoughts, or feelings.

Symbolism

A curse can be viewed as a burden, and right from the start, it is placed
upon this child. The age of sixteen is a critical time when a girl is expected
to become a woman, which is the moment the curse is activated. We may
wake in the middle of the night, beckoned by latent needs of the deeper
self, yet sometimes we stay in slumber. Perhaps out of need, a part of us
may require we be with the dark, a symbolic act of 'cocooning.' Cocooning
has a healing aspect and, as with everything we have seen, a shadow aspect.
Cocooning gives us time to be with the parts of self that feel slighted,
rejected, or abandoned, a powerful reprieve from what has us bound up
within a challenging phase of life. Yet with the shadow of cocooning, we
can become bitter, isolated, and resentful and go unconscious or become
numb. Numbness and silence parallel one another in this landscape. We
must have discernment and ask ourselves if we are cocooning to rest and
regenerate, or to escape and remain frozen; are we sleeping to rest and
heal or because we seek an out, a way to disappear?

The king and queen attempt to eliminate the perceived threat. This is what the ego does; the dominating principle within the psyche tries to take control to help us avoid suffering. The princess waits in her state of slumber, hoping for the kiss of life that will bring her home to herself. Sleeping Beauty is still cocooning; unable to awaken on her own, she needs an external force to help her. She is silenced.

Silence can be a form of numbness, a paralysis of the voice, the expression, and our authentic nature. The shadow of the things we could not, cannot, or refuse to express. Whether through force or choice, the restriction of the authentic voice is liberated as we reclaim what was silent or silenced. The silent, still, heavy places within can begin showing signs of life, including gurgling, fluttering, and spaciousness. What was once numb may start to awaken. An escape need not come from outside numbness; it is offered in the darkness itself.

New rituals emerge, ideas break into consciousness, and energy is free to move in ways it never could before. The darkness holds gifts. To accept them, we may need to descend into uncomfortable places and face the stories tucked within our tissues and turbulent memories. The prince may reflect the solar return of masculine energy. It is not a literal man that comes to her but the internal presence of power she embodies that brings her back to life. The kiss need not be physical but can be the spark of revelation, a spiritual realization, or aha moment that allows us to elevate a perspective.

To understand this is to move beyond the fixed idea of man and woman and understand the energetic principles of solar and lunar, yin and yang consciousness. The merging of these energies is the sacred marriage, the union of opposites, and polar energies, a Jungian concept rooted in alchemical studies. As the psyche works on our behalf repeatedly, it uses images and themes to move these forms from the shadow (unconscious) into the light of being (ego awareness).

Your Turn: Numb

Not all sleep is restorative. Sometimes, we put ourselves under—in sleep, substance, or story—to go unconscious for some reprieve from the all-too-muchness of life. Expanding capacity to be with sensations impacts our ability to hold other experiences, moving beyond the transmutation of pain and into the richness of enchantment, magic, and joy. Once we no longer fear our darkness, we can open to deeper dimensions of being. We must enter the places we fear, turn toward the darkness, and respect the body, the feminine, and the places that have lost life. We then awaken the places and spaces that have been frozen in time.

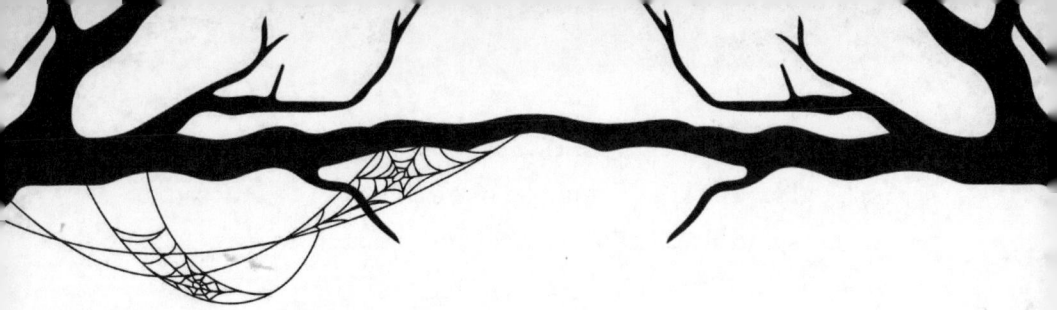

Journal Prompts

What part(s) of you feels numb or frozen in time?

Is there an aspect of self that feels dead to you? Have you numbed out a moment, memory, or sensation that seems too big to feel?

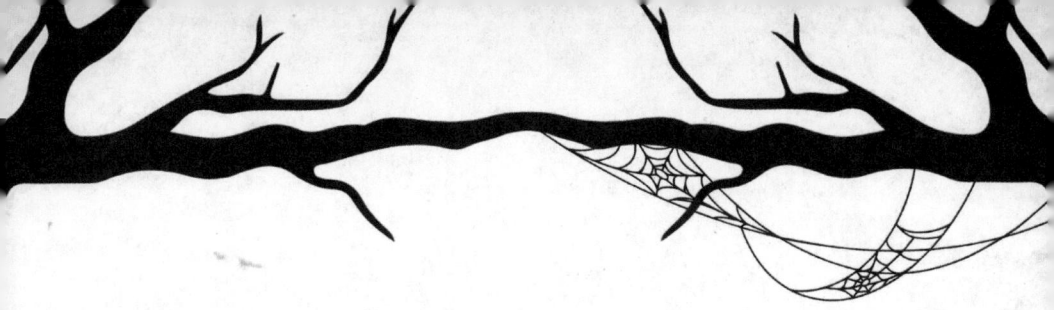

What sends you into numbness or slumber? What makes you ice people out and leave them in the cold?

~~~~~~

~~~~~~

~~~~~~

~~~~~~

~~~~~~

Sit with the symbols of ice and numbness in body or mind, free write on it in your darkness journal, and see what wisdom wants to come out of the wound.

~~~~~~

~~~~~~

~~~~~~

~~~~~~

~~~~~~

~~~~~~

Reflection

This chapter described the paradoxical nature of numbness—the seeming absence of feeling that conceals potent psychic energy. *Sleeping Beauty* speaks to how one can be emotionally or spiritually "asleep," or cut off from life, sometimes as a form of protection. The glass child and aspects of the frozen psyche teach us that what appears cold or numb may be undergoing a slow and intentional transformation. As we thaw, we reconnect with lost aspects of the self and awaken our capacity for deeper feeling and expression. Notice what is thawing out, coming to life... give it more life by writing about it now...

07

CHAPTER

Decomposed

She Who
Breaks Down

eath and decay teach us how to allow parts of ourself to break down or die off as new aspects are born. Through death, our matter (mater/earth/mother) returns to the earth. Ritual is embedded in decay and decomposition. Carl Jung believed there was an invisible bridge between the psyche and soma. He called this the psychoid, a link between the soul, the body, and the natural world. It is neither purely psychological nor purely biological but a liminal realm where the two overlap. Jung saw it as the foundation of archetypal patterns, a deep layer of the unconscious that influences both mind and matter. This concept aligns with synchronicity, suggesting that psyche and world are not separate but interconnected through this deeper layer of reality. The natural world often provides us with processes to recognize the interconnectedness of all things.

Time with nature provides comfort while we contend with matters of decomposition and decay. This gives us access to the wisdom within the circumstances that seem to be breaking down. With nature, we intuitively enter an intangible space where the visible (known ways and ideas) and invisible (unmanifest potential and divine intelligence) discretely touch one another.

On the surface, sacrifice, intuition, and decay seem to have nothing in common. Our defenses can decompose and break down, and as this occurs, it may require a great sacrifice. We may need to become more aware, more conscious, and attuned to the secret patterns of our lives. This may cause us to see what was once denied or retrieve what has been projected upon another. We may be asked to sacrifice our comforts to gain validation for our deeper knowings. This type of decay takes a willingness to let things go, regardless of how much we cherish their presence.

In my experience, these elements coalesced as I observed and interacted with the natural world. The woods were a comforting home, the place where I received nurturing, the place where I brought my heavy heart and burdens. I learned to receive love from the woods and dark hollows of the forest. I also learned not to fear death yet see it as an integral part of life.

Fallen trees decompose, breaking down and returning to the soil. When an animal dies, the flesh falls away and the soft tissue is consumed. Insects and other creatures support the process. As gruesome as it may be to some, this process has its own intelligence. The sun bleaches the bones as they sit, patiently awaiting the next step. Perhaps scattered by another creature or the wind, the bones continue to decay and eventually become brittle, as they sink down into the earth.

To explore the natural world is to enter a collaboration with the unseen world—yet we must remove the literal from the locale and drop into the metaphorical. Why do some turn away from a rotting log while others move in closer? Some see an opening in the earth and are excited to explore and investigate; others fear what might be hiding there, are cautious, and step back slowly. We should trust our instinctive draw to nature. When we contemplate with presence, we can better understand what we notice through our reflections on the natural world. When we stop noticing and fail to be a part of the natural world, we disrupt our relationship with nature. This split can manifest in neurosis.

We might be surprised at what arises from shadow as we navigate change or transition between one way of being and the next. Decomposition and decay are ultimately expressions of change. We can spot them as we turn toward our lives and get brutally honest about the quality of our experiences. How do we really feel about a career, a relationship, or a draining circumstance? We must be willing to explore darkness and shadow, to symbolically enter the forest and engage with the dark side of our human nature. Then, we become unapologetic toward our intolerance of the behaviors that seek to tame us. We must stop sacrificing our intuition and inner knowing to make others more comfortable. If we do not use our instincts, they will start to decay.

We cannot venture into the wild without coalescing with death or decay. They are natural processes—as life ends, signs of decomposition mark a transition. Nature is in a constant ouroboric state of creation and destruction. Mushrooms transform decaying wood into humus, tending to the living and dying earth. From the forest floor to the shadow, decay may warn of decomposition within an individual, revealing a breakdown of health and the presence of sickness: a disintegration, division, separation, reduction, and distillation.

Emotionally, decay may relate to memory fading throughout time or the breakdown of a personality or psychological construct. As the self withdraws and begins to decay, it loses aspects of its being, traits, qualities, or inhibited behaviors due to impactful moments or trauma. Psychological decomposition is a response to a stressor the individual can no longer respond or cope with in current circumstances, and they then become vulnerable to unconscious elements experienced as a form of psychic disturbance.

This is not as terrible as it sounds. Our bodies are finely attuned to the rhythms and cycles of nature—the moon, the cosmos, and the ever-changing seasons, and we must stop apologizing for it. The fire never apologizes for its light nor for burning things down. We must not apologize when parts of us break down. Every aspect of decay and decomposition—suppressed feelings, forgotten memories, or emotions surfacing from hidden places—serves as compost. Energetic and emotional debris has a purpose. Decay teaches us how to be with darkness and endings.

Compost is churned every time we face a fear, listen to the soul over the external world, and move inward instead of falling for the relentless distractions that compete for our attention. We sharpen and awaken instincts, attuning our senses and enhancing abilities to avoid danger and engage more fully in life. Tracking and tracing our patterns invites us to discover how and why we break down, and how we come to know death in its various forms. The psychological death of the ego can abruptly force us to face our edges, ensuring we become acclimated to discomfort and enter the unknown. This requires us to walk the thresholds of new territory, the dark forests, or caverns of our lives.

Shadow work allows us to move through a decaying situation and find meaning. Honoring the stirrings and unsettled musings brings us back in touch with what we have suppressed, allowing new life to emerge in deadened spaces. Confronting our aversions, we open to the depths of the true self. These moments require deep listening, silence, and distance from the obligations and expectations of daily life. The imagination is activated in stillness. Paradoxically, bringing awareness to the night, dreams, and the unconscious can regenerate disintegrating hopes, intentions, or dreams.

At night, when all is quiet, dreadful feelings may find their way into the mind. The psyche does not stop engaging simply because it is nighttime; darkness is a time of incubation. Incubation is where we go when we are fighting our growing pains, healing from an illness, or undergoing an ego death.

The dark night of the soul is a form of ego death, and the process takes form in unusual and unexpected ways. Navigating one of my darkest times revealed a difficult and stubborn pattern, a power struggle that unconsciously required me to give my power over to others to gain their trust and friendship. We experience a chaos of the mind, a depression, or find ourselves descending back into the underworld—all showing us we have an ego amid a necessary crisis.

As we move through the dark night, like in the fairy tale, the animals come to guide us. They may appear in dreams, thoughts, and sometimes our backyards; they invoke feelings, reveal psychological movements, and express feelings that do not always have words. Synchronicities arrive like impulses from the universe, revealing the interconnected nature of all things.

The dark night, symbolic of the underworld, arises during challenge and struggle. The spiritual and psychological veils part as the unconscious speaks, and we gather symbolic glimpses of it in synchronistic moments. Shadow work can relieve suffering, yet it will not coddle us through change nor stop us from enduring the darkness of the natural world or human nature.

I discovered this through an unexpected (and unwanted) transformational process of observing death, followed by decomposition and decay. It was during a relentless dark night period when I witnessed a gruesome demonstration of decomposition as the vultures swooped in to clear the remnants of a creature that had unsuccessfully attempted to cross the street. As the disturbing encounter unfolded, part of me wanted to turn away, yet to my discomfort, I intuitively knew it was important I hold my gaze.

Reluctantly I sat still and watched as four vultures moved in a unified cadence, spreading their wings in reverence as if in a ceremony to honor the dead. I watched as these massive creatures perched upon a nearby roof while their target lay motionless beneath them. All four vultures slowly got closer, looming over the body, swaying, and flexing their wings.

I felt like I was their audience, observing the story they told, independent of anything my mind could conjure or project on them. My mind rushed to make this moment mean something, to give form to nature's disturbing yet divine design. As the creatures got to work devouring the dead, a part of me wanted to soften the odd somatic sensation circling my heart and soothe my squeamish stomach; their movements mimicked my inner sensations. I refrained from making assumptions about the methodical gestures of the vultures.

Vultures are portrayed as predators. We judge the grotesque nature of their habits and feeding rituals, pacifying the discomfort of confronting dark things such as death and decay. Vultures are not creatures who kill. They are large birds that do the dirty work, instinctively devouring the dead and preventing the spread of disease, a realization that can feel cathartic when applied metaphorically.

By remaining open and present to this event, I could see the decaying aspects of my life, a deep recognition that it was time to let go of a few things. Witnessing the vultures created an unexpected cathartic response. After reflecting, my intuition alerted me to find the value in the observation: the restraint I demonstrated by not giving in to the ego as it wished to get beyond the grim occurrence and the power of presence. The vultures were an example of witnessing nature's naked, raw reflections.

Following the thread of raw reflections, it feels significant to address something here. Unfortunately, there are moments when we are cut off from other parts, and we succumb to the unconscious impulses of our wounding. I, like many others, am deeply acquainted with the impact suicide leaves behind and the enormous loss of the one who departed. This is a vast subject; I only feel called to illustrate one perspective on suicide. It is safe to assume those who are suicidal or have ended their life are likely in a state of suffering. What I wish they could have known is the interworking of the psyche. They may have discovered that they didn't necessarily want to die; they wanted to kill off the parts of themselves that felt the pain, that suffered in the pattern or cycle, the parts of themselves that could no longer hold their emotional burden(s).

The word ritual comes from an Indo-European root meaning "to fit together." Observing the vultures in action allowed a psychological assembly of ritual, insight, and reflection, all ingredients fitting together the pieces to tend to the soul. To deny death is not to defy it. We cannot escape death, although we can learn to honor it, remembering that even dying stars decompose, shedding their outer layers. Moving into the depths and working with the shadow realms includes ritual and ceremony. Rituals offer a way through painful stages to believe there is a latent meaning within an experience. Ceremonies honor transitional moments, demarcating an experience regardless of how we view it.

The cadence of the vultures put me into a trance, and their simple movements activated something in me. For a moment, I felt liberated from the disdain of being human as I observed this primitive instinctual reflection, seeing the vultures as they were in their natural state. This pure state of observation speaks to our conscious mind while giving space for unconscious elements—the unseen world within all things.

Although my eyes were open and I was present, something else was occurring. This was a reorientation with nature and the natural state of all things in their simplicity, independent of projections, kitschy descriptions, or googled animal totem meanings. The experience with the vultures was not earth-shattering; the moment could have easily been overlooked; the shadow work unfolded as I gathered each piece of insight from the interaction.

After this visitation, I spent time reflecting and journaling about the vultures. Meanings were not forced yet uncovered over time through recording dreams and with introspection. Engaging with the vulture situation required discipline while cultivating my detached observation skills and refraining from projecting meaning. The unconscious appears in wild places governed by nature yet untouched by another. The medicine is in the untouched reflection. We see more when we try less to make something more significant.

These moments of unease are messengers, not to glorify or literalize, but to witness the raw potential of unconscious material moving about the psyche. To explore decay is to heed the opportunity within nature, to shapeshift out of the artificial world of human distraction, and, with precision, direct focus back to the primal instinctive nature of all things.

The gifts from the underworld present to us as we individuate and find our way back to wholeness, providing insight into an underlying orchestrating principle within the psyche. Observing processes of death and decay is one way to reclaim the self and retrieve lost parts. There is persistence and perseverance under the work of shadow and nature, along with an innate sense of finally finding our place in the wild. Some parts of us deeply resonate with these concepts, while others tend to dismiss them, giving us an out from having to go any deeper. It serves to remember that the words 'scared' and 'sacred' contain the same letters.

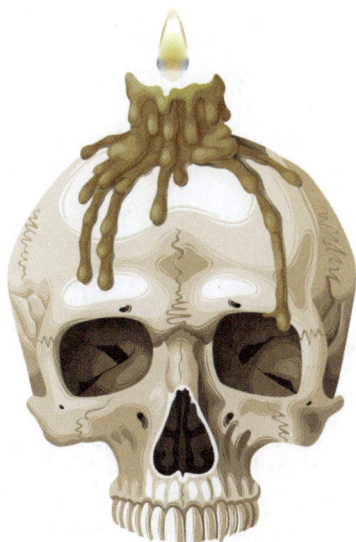

The Fairy Tale: The Girl Without Hands

It started with a deal. Once upon a time, a poor miller, desperate for money, made a bargain he didn't understand with the devil. The man in black had come to him at dusk, standing at the edge of the millpond, his voice as smooth as oil. "I'll make you rich," he had promised. "All I want is what's behind your mill."

The miller shrugged, and slowly nodded and agreed without a second thought. He should have looked first. Because standing just behind the mill, barefoot in the dirt, was his daughter. The money came—more than the miller had ever dreamed—but wealth is worthless when the devil comes to collect.

Three days later, the man in black returned. He stepped inside the house without knocking, his presence sucking the warmth from the air. His eyes settled on the girl, standing frozen near the hearth, her hands still dusted with flour.

He reached for her. And stopped. He flinched back, in fury. Something in her—something untouched, something clean—burned him like fire. Purity. Innocence. The devil could not take her as she was. Her purity protected her.

But he could change that. "Dirty her," he ordered. "Make her mine." The miller's stomach knotted. He tried, God help him, he tried. He forced her hands into filth and smeared them with the blood of a slaughtered lamb. But she washed them clean, again and again and again, until they bled.

The devil came back, each time angrier. This time, he insists her father chop off her hands.

"Cut them off," he hissed. "If she has no hands, she cannot wash them." The miller refused but the devil laughed. The gold in the house turned to rot, the miller's crops withered overnight, and the water in the well turned black.

The miller was a coward, but he was not a fool. He knew what happened to men who broke deals. So, he took his daughter outside. He did not look at her face. And he raised the axe. She screamed when the blade came down. She screamed as her father collapsed, weeping, clutching his own stomach like he was the one who had been mutilated. She screamed as the blood poured from her severed wrists, pooling in the dirt, soaking into the earth like an offering.

The miller obeyed, and the girl lost her hands. The devil reached for her one last time and still, he could not take her. Because even now—bleeding, broken—she did not belong to him. She cried and cried onto her bloody stumps. Despite the mutilation, the innocence of her tears purified her, and the devil was unsuccessful. He left her there and so, she ran.

She ran until the trees swallowed her whole, until she could no longer hear her father's sobs behind her. She ran until the ground blurred beneath her feet, until the loss of blood made the world sway and bend at the edges. She ran until she collapsed in the king's garden, where he found her in the morning.

The king was young, lonely, and kind. He was moved by her innocence and took her in. He fed her, clothed her, and protected her. And then, he married her. The king had silver hands forged just for her. They gleamed like moonlight, like armor, like something meant to replace what had been stolen. For the first time in a long while, she was safe. They lived happily for a time and were thrilled to welcome a child —happy that is until the devil found her again.

The king was away when it happened. The devil, not yet defeated, forged letters to deceive the king, leading him to believe the queen and their newborn child were dead. The child was barely a day old when the message arrived. A letter, telling of her death, and the death of their child. He did not know the letters were lies. The queen was not dead, but she sensed the devil was on his way, so she fled.

Heartbroken, the queen left with her baby, wandering again into the wilderness. She knew what was happening. She had seen enough of the devil's work to recognize it. She found sanctuary in a cottage and raised her child in peace.

The king, discovering the devil's deceit, searched for his wife and child for many years. The queen, meanwhile, grew something new. She learned to live without silver hands, without royal halls, without anyone. Through the trials, the queen's hands were miraculously restored.

Not silver. Flesh. Bone. Real. She was whole again.

She had done what the devil never expected. She had survived him. The king found her years later, and the truth unraveled. The devil had played his last game. The family returned to the kingdom—not to rule, but to rebuild. The miller, her father was gone. The devil, too. But she was still here. And in the end, that was enough.

*What did you see, sense, or feel as you
read The Girl Without Hands?*

Check in with your body, go to your darkness journal, and write down
any initial impressions, thoughts, or feelings.

Symbolism

A 'Faustian bargain' is a deal with the devil. Some deals are made
unconsciously, sacrificing parts of us in service to something better,
newer, enhanced, or enchanted. Although there is a sense of helplessness
here as the young girl cries out, in her suffering and tears, her innocence
protects her. We have an opportunity here to remember our states
of wholeness, independent of perfection. We must confront our
unconscious enabling of purity culture, which tries to cleanse and clear
anything less than acceptable; this is a form of psychological mutilation.
This pattern informs us the ego is operating, not the soul.

Interestingly, the girl must leave home for her process to fully engage,
symbolizing the necessity of leaving the comfort of familiar places,
especially those that cause us to sacrifice parts of ourselves to remain
there. We can become stagnant and emotionally decompose if we stay
where we do not belong. This story is not meant to draw attention
to the figure of the father so we can blame the literal father, but the
metaphorical masculine principle, the part of us that is tethered to an

invisible paradigm controlling our innate sense of value and worth. They are the stories we tell ourselves about why and how we matter.

In this sense, the devil may be a compulsion or affliction, the part of us that emerges when we refuse to tend to the shadow and look closer into the cycles and rituals operating beneath consciousness; a complex that creates chaos, cuts us into pieces and forces us to comply. The devil forges letters to the king; we may see this as hidden elements (the unconscious) trying to take over and fool the ego (consciousness). The king is often the ego in a fairy tale, the governing or ruling principle.

To restore the hands is to bring back essential elements that have been 'out of touch,' or unable to 'grab hold of something.' The return of the hands can also signify the return of her own power and strength in her femininity—pure, innocent, whole, and complete—as she always has been before life brought her through these various decompositions and periods of decay. There is a necessity in death, whether we are willing or not to embrace it. As the old breaks down, we can learn to trust it will be replaced by something new, or we may embody a new principle, belief, or quality. Faith in our instincts can be restored. We sacrifice the story we wanted for a deeper truth to emerge. This might mean we see something or someone for who they are, not for who we hope they will be.

Your Turn: Decomposing

Not all observations are pleasant and joyful; nature demonstrates without censorship, inviting us to step back from our carefully curated, safe worlds. Although we seek to protect and shield ourselves from the unknown phases, dark moments, and uncomfortable experiences, they are just as sacred and profound. Sometimes the kindest act is death, allowing something to die, to rest in peace, and open psychic and emotional space for something new. What once was will now change its form as it breaks down. Parts of us die to birth new aspects.

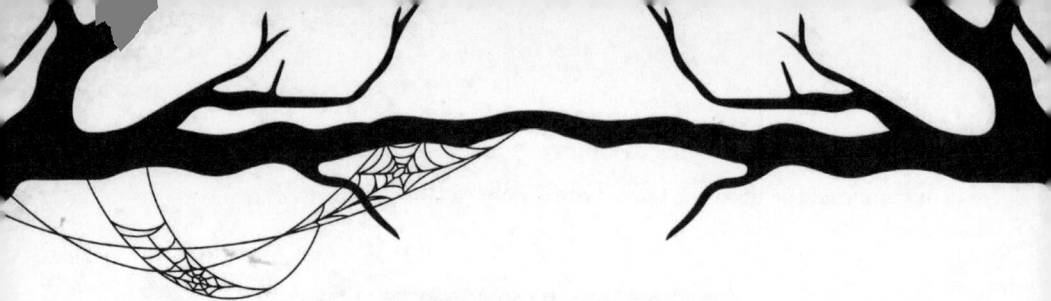

Journal Prompts

How do you break down what happens to you emotionally? Is there an aspect of self that needs to die off?

Have you ever made a deal with the devil (think symbolically not literally)? How did it work out, what was the lesson?

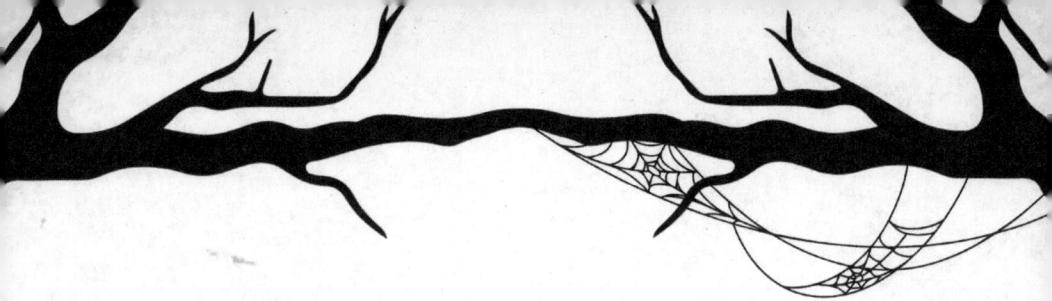

What scares you about decomposing and/or dying?

Sit with a part of you that is actively dying (i.e., a belief, relationship, or a part of your identity) and free write on it in your darkness journal, and see what wisdom wants to come out of the wound.

Reflection

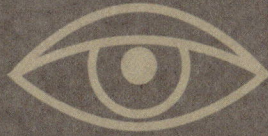

This chapter attunes us to the themes of decomposition, decay, and death. Breaking down has value, and things that make us uncomfortable are not always as frightening as they appear on the surface. *The Girl Without Hands* illuminates how mutilation leads to redemption and regeneration. Her return to wholeness is earned, not given freely. What dies becomes soil for what is to come. Contemplate these ideas, breathe new life into them as you write...

08
CHAPTER

Deceived

She Who Is Hunted

Monsters. We fear them; we project our horrors upon them. Giving them power, we declare them formidable forces with a touch of supernatural swagger—the inverted hero, the villain, the dark night. We imagine them stalking in shadow, terrorizing the vulnerable. We fear what we do not understand, not understanding why we are so afraid. We invest our time and energy in fighting, stopping, and keeping them at a distance. We lie and tell ourselves they exist, but in a faraway land, a headline in a newspaper, the bogeyman in someone else's nightmare.

As time passes, our language has changed. Monsters have been replaced by narcissists and psychopaths. The danger here is how quickly these terms have become kitschy words, normalized by our inability to be with darkness. We strive to be more and to have more, convinced that 'more' is the answer. We are vulnerable to our own appetites, yet this is cleverly disguised. Hidden behind the relentless pursuit and the obtainment of achievement is our fear of a greater monster we call mediocrity. The antipathy of being ordinary or unremarkable tricks people into believing accomplishments can foster fulfillment, a misconception that contributes to normalizing narcissism.

A prime directive of depth psychology is to make what is unconscious more conscious, tapping into the archetypal basis of the mind: the patterns personified as Gods. The myth points us to dangers hidden in plain sight. Narcissus fell into the water, chasing his reflection, infatuated with his image. This psychological symbol is activated as the fear of being ordinary nudges us closer to the pond's edge.

Suddenly, everyone is a narcissist or knows one, but when will we address our own narcissism? Although there is great truth in the increase in narcissism, there is a different type of beastly issue hiding in the background. This beast is our fear of depth, the dark, watery, unknown spaces within us, and the terrifying possibility that we may not be much different than the madman or the murderer. We fear our capacity to do horrible things. Working with the imaginal requires us to tend to the hidden and meet the monsters of the mind, befriending our beasts.

> The shadow holds it all for us—the terrible thoughts, the disturbing possibilities, the parts of us we dare not show or expose. Our destructive tendencies, our wishes to kill off, to stifle, to keep others from rising. Our jealous rage and hatred toward 'otherness.'

The term monster meant 'to warn or remind.' Some cultures believed monsters were an omen, here to warn us of potential danger, disaster, or deception. In myth, these figures were depicted as creatures, those who held our attention through either attraction or aversion, a simultaneously unsettling sense. This theme is present in myself and those who tend to be drawn to my work. We are the ones who cannot look away, regardless of how horrific the scene may be; in fact, we are the weirdos who try to gain some ground and get a little closer. Monsters can humble us, hunting our triggers and forcing us to meet our own madness.

My curiosity about death and darkness began early. With lots of time spent alone, my favorite childhood game was playing detective, roaming the woods around my home searching for evidence, turning over stones, and digging in the dirt along the forest floor. I felt driven by a compulsion to search, seek out, and look beneath objects. I was convinced I would solve a crime by finding a dead body, never considering where these thoughts came from or how this game began.

In a bizarre and synchronistic occurrence, a serial killer had dumped a pair of legs in the river down the road from my home. I was in elementary school at the time and decided to bring the newspaper clipping of the article to school one day for 'show and tell.' Each student would stand in front of the class with an item, and they had to discuss it. My presentation was not well received. Later that day, my mom sat me down to explain why my teacher was upset and that these types of things were not appropriate to bring to school.

Decades later, I found out that a relative (an actual detective) had attended the scene where the body parts were found. There were other synchronicities. Several years after my show-and-tell incident, my mother sat me down and explained another hair-raising story. A second serial killer had murdered five people and was connected to more than 200 deaths. Not only was it disturbing to discover that body parts were found near my home, but then she informed me that a family friend was a victim of the serial killer. These events

somehow, oddly, validated something. I was only a teenager, yet these events ignited a deep desire within me.

I am not interested in glorifying serial killers; I feel we can learn from the behaviors and rituals of deeply disturbed individuals. I once read a quote by Kenneth Tynan that haunted me in the best way possible: "We seek the teeth to match our wounds." Wounds are apertures, openings that allow material to move into the surface of conscious awareness. Viewing wounds mythically opens hidden meaning; like portals, they allow us to assimilate and transmute stored emotions.

While conducting some research, I came across a recording from a relative of convicted serial killer Ted Bundy. She was around him for many years, and her mother had a relationship with him. She admitted to hiding a letter from Ted that was intended for her mother at the time Ted was on death row. When asked why she hid the letter from her mother, she responded, "She's got a piece of her that responds to him, and I didn't want to see that piece exploited again." Emotionally speaking, he had the teeth that matched her wounds.

In a dark twist of events, I discovered that Ted Bundy was linked to a specific piece of forensic evidence: his teeth were matched to bite marks found on one of his victims. These pieces all came together in an uncanny symbolic manner—teeth to match the wounds. These details hit my gut; intuitively, I began tracing these elements. This was an example of a psychological pattern, the blind spot within, when someone on the outside can see more clearly than we can. We are at the whim of our afflictions, and the more we try to separate ourselves from darkness, the more it will unconsciously grip us.

The pattern behind the action is essential, the psychological incongruence within the shadow and psyche that makes us vulnerable to people such as this deeply disturbed and afflicted individual. Justice permeates the psyche of many women, nudging them to seek out truth. To do so, we are often called to look at disturbances, anomalies, or things that just seem off about a person or situation. We look at afflictions as a secret portal into the shadow.

The hauntingly beautiful etymology of the word affliction comes from the Greek word *kakopatheo*; breaking it apart, we have *kakos* and *pathos*: evil and suffering. It's critical to assess ideas about evil with a neutral context, rather than a projection of fear. With fear, we unconsciously place hidden beliefs upon the subjects, topics, and concepts we consider evil, adding the burden of responsibility to what we do not know how to face. Therefore, affliction is not evil in the typical sense. In Aramaic, the word evil means 'unripe.' Perhaps all things have their own innate time of becoming.

Fearing the dark, we imprint it with our demons, misinterpreting the unknown as evil and projecting our imagined mental horrors upon it, fearing what we may see, sense, or feel if we get too close. We know from following the narrative of any good fairy tale that this denial of the dark only ensures it will meet us upon the path. The shadow cannot be contained or described completely; no archetypal construct within the psyche can, yet we can consider the many expressions of the shadow by discerning our individual images as we experience them in dreams, sensations, feelings, and reactions. It is a unique and personal experience of how they borrow each moment and interlace with the shadow and self. The psyche will metaphorically paint a doorway if one cannot be found, a perpetual endeavor of reinvention through creation and destruction.

The dormant function of intuition comes alive as we interact with the many faces of deception. These are core wounds many of us will endure at some point. These core wounds are rejection, abandonment, humiliation, and betrayal. The darker fairy tales contain this hidden potential, which is easy to miss at first glance. We can learn from fairy tales to make peace with unfavorable behaviors to uncover and discern those who do not operate with integrity. As the tales unfold, deeper archetypal patterns reveal the deceptive intentions of characters or creatures. Reading the tale is a way of externalizing the pattern, a safe distancing so we may begin locating our own vulnerabilities.

Within a fairy tale, deceit is not merely a device for creating conflict or drama, it is a mirror of tricky behaviors and attitudes that most of us would rather not admit exist. Whether in the self or another, these behaviors challenge us to reflect and consider moral values and the consequences of our actions, even more so the deeper implications of certain personalities that have common ego defenses built into their responses and interactions with others.

Deceit in fairy tales plays a significant role in developing intuition, teaching discernment through the process of sifting and sorting, and helping us parse out truth from lies in forms we can see more clearly. It is easier to define the cage once we have freed ourselves from it. Deceit forces moral complexity into fairy tales, demanding both characters and the one who reads the tale to confront their blind spots. Creatures, people, and formidable forces appear on the path. False promises, acts of betrayal, and seemingly unnecessary cruelty litter the story with dramatic and horrific ideas. Here we are, unable to escape the terrors that stand before us.

Creatures appear out of nowhere, offering advice, support, or a heroic act, only for us to discover that they were never who we believed them to be. We have no choice but to look beyond the surface of an interaction and come back to the intuition to discern deeper truths and motivations. As characters deceive or are deceived, we experience a range of emotions, from unyielding rage to utter hopelessness and betrayal. This emotional pursuit is crucial in developing a nuanced understanding of human relationships, enhancing one's ability to intuitively read emotional cues and underlying intentions in real-life interactions.

Fairy tales sometimes end with a positive resolution, yet we are not guaranteed to live happily ever after. Deceit is not always punished, and honesty is not always rewarded; we get to confront the nuances of truth and integrity. Consequences of deceitful behavior do not always end in victory, yet they are always there. Even if buried within the psyche, there is a response or ripple created from an action. Sometimes, this is the truth we must hold onto when justice has not or cannot be served.

The intuitive and compassionate ones must learn they are here to break the spell, to release the projections of those who deny their disparate shadow aspects and cast them on the deeply feeling and sensitive ones. They are scapegoats, the ones who shoulder the unconscious burdens. Even the black sheep were chosen for that role unconsciously by those who put them in that position with their projections. They always belonged, just in a different form. The black sheep and scapegoat are duty-bound. They unknowingly have been called to unpack the layers of expectations placed upon them; this is part of holding and containing darkness for others. They are catalysts for change, meant to disrupt familial, ancestral, and cultural patterns.

When we orient to the light and are fearful or dismissive of the dark, we become vulnerable to the predatory nature of other creatures. In depth psychology, we are taught to remain in purposeful tension with opposites—dark and light, solar and lunar, seen and unseen, order and chaos. The solar qualities represent the known, the conscious, the illuminated self, while the lunar qualities pull us toward the unknown, the hidden, the unconscious. But just as we can be blind to our own shadow, we can also be blinded by the light—entranced by false security, unable or unwilling to see what lurks in the darkness. A fixation on light is not enlightenment—it is an illusion, a deception of its own. To reject the dark entirely is to weaken our ability to recognize danger, to sense the predator when it is near.

This dangerous pattern caught me in a loop, surrounded by others put off by my desire to study darkness; they were uncomfortable with my interest in all things unusual and macabre. They began distancing themselves while simultaneously tossing positive platitudes about love, light, and thinking positively my way. They were determined to help me "raise my vibration" and focus on the good, all modes of utilizing toxic positivity and spiritual bypassing to avoid the depths.

This is the shadow, a form of artificial light, something I have come to call light culture—a belief system that clings desperately to positivity, purity, and safety while leaving the monsters and darkness for others to deal with. Toxic positivity and spiritual bypassing are not merely naive—they are dangerous. They allow wolves to walk among us, unchallenged and unseen.

True awareness does not look away. It does not soften what is sharp or shield us from what is monstrous. If we are genuinely seeking truth and following our soul's path, we will inevitably unsettle someone—agitating, appalling, and even repulsing them. If no one is disturbed, we may not be authentically seeking on behalf of the self but merely appeasing the ego.

Intuition is a tool for navigating darkness, yet if subtle cues are overwhelmed by emotion or the distraction of an archetypal complex, we may be unable to sense the still, quiet voice within and a compulsion may overcome us. This translates psychologically to being aware of our surroundings, honing deeper instincts rather than being consumed by them, and looking beyond the persona presented by another.

Avoiding the shadow weakens defenses and access to necessary information. Spiritual bypassing can hamper feelings and dismiss insights that block critical information felt or sensed when something doesn't sit right about something or someone. The alchemists set out to transform lead into gold; psychologically, this is the opus, the alchemical process of spiritually transforming the instinct. Life contains a greater sense of vibrancy as the instincts are transformed, and the ego reorients toward the self. Staying with the intensity presented by darkness allows something to brew; we lose this if we are too quick to escape the moment.

If we grow up within a toxic environment, the psychological torment of emotional disturbance changes the brain, and our natural defenses adapt as needed. It is traumatic never to know who to trust or to anticipate the next move of an erratic or disturbed individual. The sensitive ones are often the scapegoats and take the brunt of these patterns. It takes time to heal the distorted lens one sees through living this way. The wounds are not visible, and it can feel as if you are living under a spell, and, in a way, you are, possibly dissociated, and likely in a disempowered state. Instead of questioning the other, we question ourselves.

Those who survive the ordeals of deceit and deception will birth a form of sight that has nothing to do with the physical eyes. You return with a keen sense of the human condition, begin to cut through the noise, can detect discordance immediately, and your tolerance for superficial charm diminishes. Your survival brings out shadow abilities, gifts that were either buried, hidden, or dismissed. As you return, you and everyone around you can sense and feel the shift; you are no longer the person who entered the dark forest.

The Fairy Tale: Little Red Riding Hood

The girl had always been called Little Red Riding Hood, though nobody remembered why. Maybe it was the cloak, the deep blood-red fabric she wore no matter the season. That morning, her mother handed her a basket of food, a bottle of wine, and a warning: "Go straight to your grandmother's. Don't talk to anyone. Stay on the path." Little Red Riding Hood nodded, but she wasn't really listening.

She should have listened. She crossed the river and made her way deep into the forest. The path was long, the woods were quiet, and the wolf was waiting. She didn't know this creature, but he knew a lot about her, including her vulnerabilities and insecurities. The wolf was confident and extremely charming, yet something seemed off.

There was something in his grin that made her stomach turn—too many teeth, too much patience. The smile felt hollow and empty. She felt a pang of guilt for judging this stranger. "Where are you going, little girl?" Red hesitated, then gripped the basket tighter. "To my grandmother's." She saw it then—the flicker of something in his eyes, calculating. "What a good girl you are."

She left before he could say more, her pulse quickening, the woods suddenly darker than before. She didn't see him watching her. She didn't see him turn and slip away, moving faster than any creature should.

Little Red Riding Hood arrives at her grandmother's house and knocks. Her grandmother lived alone, but she always answered the door. Not this time. No answer.

She knocked again. Still nothing. The door swung open on its own.

Inside, the house was too still, too quiet. Something reeked—a deep, metallic scent that clung to the air. "Grandmother?" The figure in the bed shifted. Something was wrong. Little Red Riding Hood felt it in her body, but she talked herself out of feeling the dread that filled the room.

Little Red Riding Hood knew the shape of her grandmother—the gentle frame, the soft shoulders, the way she smelled like bread and lavender. But the thing in the bed was not her grandmother. It was too big. Too still. Its breath was too slow, too deep. Watching. Waiting.

She stepped closer, heart hammering, gripping the basket like a weapon. "Grandmother, what big eyes you have." The thing in the bed didn't blink. "To see you better, my dear." The voice was low, thick, wrong.

Little Red Riding Hood took another step. "Grandmother, what big ears you have." A sharp inhale. The covers shifted. "To hear you better." Her stomach curled. The smell was stronger now. She swallowed. "Grandmother, what big teeth you have."

The covers slid away. A hand shot out—clawed fingers, nails like daggers. Not a hand. A paw. And then the thing lunged. The basket hit the floor, the wine bottle shatters, the dark purple liquid spilling everywhere almost in slow motion. She never had time to scream.

The weight of it crushed her and pinned her to the bed. The stench of meat and death and wet fur filled her lungs. She fought. It didn't matter. Teeth clamped down on her shoulder, her chest, her throat. Pain. And then darkness.

A man with a knife burst through the door. She didn't see the hunter step inside, his axe glinting in the dim light. She didn't hear the way he cursed when he saw the bed, the mess, the body. He had been hunting this thing for weeks. He had found it too late.

The wolf—if it was a wolf at all—was bloated, tired, and satisfied. The hunter didn't hesitate. One clean swing. Then another and another. The wolf fell as the hunter plunged the knife deep into the mass of fur and flesh. He cut deep. Blood gushed, thick and black, slicking his hands, his arms, the floor beneath him. And then a gasp. A small, wet cough. A hand trembled inside the mess of it. Not a claw. A human hand.

And then another. And then she sat up. Her skin was slick with blood, her eyes wide, unseeing. But she was breathing. Somehow, she was still breathing. The hunter pulled her from the mess, from the thing that had tried to consume her. She should have been dead. She wiped her mouth and spit something black onto the floor. Then she looked at the hunter and smiled. It was the first time she had ever smiled with teeth.

What did you see, sense, or feel as you read Little Red Riding Hood?

Check in with your body, go to your darkness journal, and write down any initial impressions, thoughts, or feelings.

Symbolism

A sweet, innocent girl finds herself at the edge of the forest (the unconscious). Edges are thresholds and powerful locations, physically and psychologically. She is on her way to her grandmother's house. Interestingly, the grandmother could represent the crone (wise one) while the young girl reflects the maiden (naive and vulnerable).

A wolf, the predator on the path, shows himself initially before pretending to be the grandmother. How often does one who is deceptive or predatory wear the clothes of a guru or leader? We must use discernment and honor our instincts. Little Red Riding Hood muffles the inner voice but knows something is incongruent here. She does not listen and is then devoured by the wolf. Our compulsions and afflictions can consume us, so we must be willing to confront our vulnerabilities instead of ignoring the dangers. If not, we may unknowingly bring them home (into the house, body, psyche).

The dangers can be toxic situations, people, thoughts, or ideas. They need not be literal; energetic forces can keep us victimized and disempowered. Appearances can sometimes fool us; some use beauty and charm to disarm us. The hunter represents support, an ally within the psyche. The hunter can be intuition, our fierce shadow stepping in on our behalf to rescue us from our demise. Redemption can come by sitting and listening, enforcing a boundary, or ferociously tearing into a matter (teeth on flesh) to reclaim innocence, sovereignty, or anything rightfully ours.

Your Turn: Deceived

Sometimes, we are preyed upon. This is not to say we created it, attracted it, or brought it to our door. Yet if we have been emotionally marked by a life-changing experience, there can be trace evidence that may leave us more vulnerable. The grooves of these events become the teeth marks upon our flesh, visible to those with malevolent intent. Sometimes, we were lured into the web of someone else's affliction or compulsion. It can be ugly, dangerous, and unfathomable, yet if you lived to tell the tale, your story does not end there. Being deceived does not mean we lack intelligence or have not been diligently working with the mind to co-create our reality. Terrible things happen, people die, and we must do our best to recover and heal, knowing there are unavoidable dangers along the way. It is the risk one takes to live more fully and authentically, which will not always be understood by those who wish to play it safe. They will never consider going into the forest to discover the deep transformative power that awaits them.

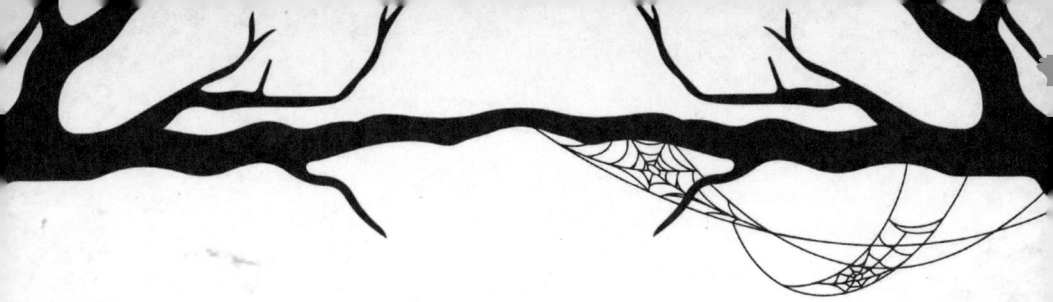

Journal Prompts

Do your monsters have a name?

....

....

....

....

....

What pattern continues to hunt you as you seek out your wounds?

....

....

....

....

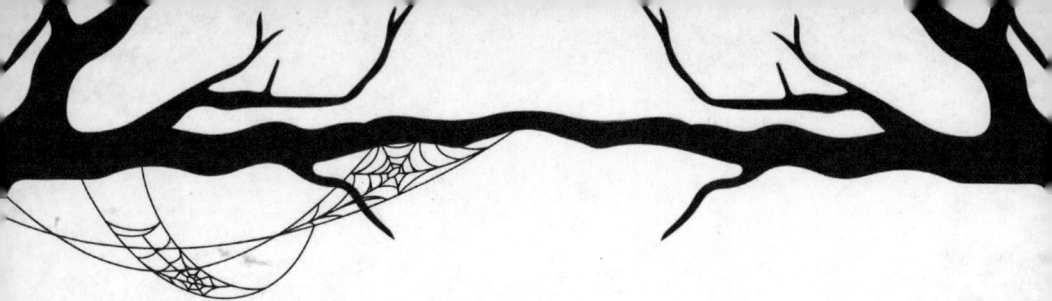

Who or what deceived you so deeply that it altered your ability to trust?

_____

_____

_____

_____

_____

_____

Is there a part of you that feels perpetually wounded or vulnerable?

_____

_____

_____

_____

_____

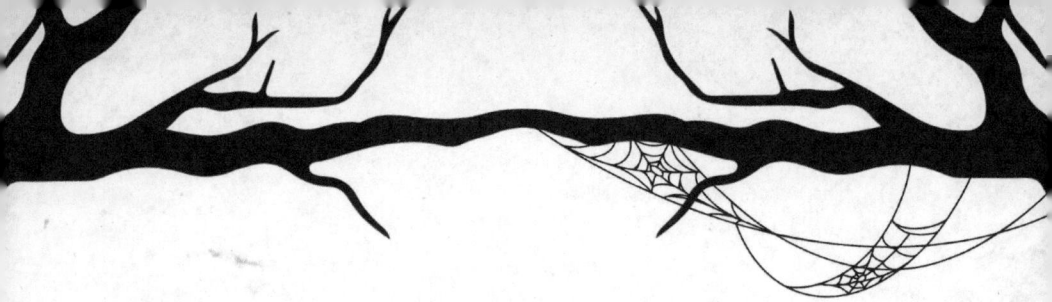

Whose teeth have matched your wounds? Free write on it in your darkness journal, and see what wisdom wants to come out of the wound.

Reflection

This chapter invites us to become mindful of the predator, not as some distant mythic beast, but as a psychic presence that stalks us in our dreams, in our choices, and in our vulnerabilities. These ideas force us to contend with deception and deceit. *Little Red Riding Hood* shows how discernment and intuition are essential aspects of psychic survival. The more we understand about darkness, the more equipped we feel to live with confidence in our instincts. How does this feel for you? Write it out here...

Deepening the Work: Integration

S hadow work is a continual process. Like the ouroboros, there is no beginning or end. There is nothing to fix, you are not broken, and you are not an ongoing project. To integrate is to embody the knowledge that once spiraled within the analytical mind down into your bones. With every shift, celebrate your progress. Reflect on the changes underway, seen or unseen.

The work you experience within these pages—working the fairy tales, peering deeply into the mirror as they reveal your inner world, writing in your darkness journal, and giving space to hold the darkest parts is not for the faint of heart. Transmuting shadow, healing, and transformation are cyclical. Each encounter has a beginning and an end, but the work continues to unfold.

Shadow work is not linear. We use the symbol of the spiral to demonstrate the nature of these energetic and innate processes. The spiral can represent patterns of growth, evolution, and movement. There is no straight path, although it would please the ego to have a clearly defined destination with specific instructions on where to go, what to do, and how to make things happen.

As you return to this book, consider which themes call to you, revisit them, yet try to come back with the attitude of listening to the psyche as she leads you to the theme you need to explore. Do your best to release the ego's desire to make things happen or to force change. It rarely ends well when the ego attempts to dominate or control the choices.

An open mind is critical for discovering new content within the shadow and the unconscious. Let things rise and fall within their natural rhythm. The shadow will help you if you let it. Only you can choose to show up with courage and face yourself with each opportunity to descend into darkness.

> We cannot defeat the shadow, yet we need not fear it either. It is a companion, a consort, and an ally on the dark path. The dark path is not always easy, but it is deeply satisfying, enriching, never boring, and filled with life the way we were meant to experience it.

Stay open, stay humble, and always trust your gut. As you continue to move within each ring of the spiral, the psyche will bring you deeper and deeper into the spaces where you get to know your soul. Making darkness conscious is the reward of shadow work, actualizing and embodying invisible light, the gold within the psyche.

If you feel called to continue working with the shadow, you can find additional training through the workshops, courses, and meditative tracks on my website. There is also a quiz on the home page to help you discover your dominant shadow function: www.melissacorter.com.

Acknowledgments

To my dear mentors, professors, and analysts: Ashok Bedi, Jeanine Canty, Emmanuel Dagher, Dylan Francisco, Sunny Dawn Johnston, and Elisabeth Pomès. You have all been imperative to the reclamation of my light and the wisdom of my darkness and held space for every part of this discovery. To my cohort: Annatova, Jordan, and Zoe, I love our tiny but mighty circle. Thank you for your guidance, mentorship, and support.

My dearest friend Grace, it's been a gift to have your friendship; thank you for always being up for co-creating some serious magic while holding shadow with me. You call me out when I need it and remind me to shine when I forget who I am. I love you dearly.

Kris, my darling husband, and Jared, my beautiful boy, there are no words to capture the love I have for both of you. You are my favorite people; I feel so damn blessed to call you family. Thank you for loving me and for the endless adventures as we continue co-creating our lives together. You have both cracked my heart wide open and taught me how to love.

About the Author

Melissa is a depth psychologist, Certified Medicolegal Investigator (Death Investigator), and international bestselling author. Her expertise revolves around the shadow side of the personality. Her unique writing style blends psychology with symbolic forms found in film, fairy tales, and forensics. Melissa is trained in traditional Jungian shadow work—the root of shadow studies.

Melissa's decades of experience include the dark night of the soul, psychopathy, and encounters with darkness. Her work often makes people uncomfortable as it draws on and celebrates the macabre, dark, and misunderstood dimensions of personality. Discover your shadow function and find out more about her work here www.melissacorter.com.

To the one who has
made it this far.

You walked with me through the dark forest, picked up the broken pieces, consumed poisoned apples, and together we entered that forbidden room. You followed the breadcrumbs, sifted and sorted, and called out your ghosts.

The hardest thing is not necessarily what we think; it's to keep looking without turning away. For many years, I numbed my emotions. It seemed easier to avoid the trauma and pain until I realized the cost of that choice. My success, joy, prosperity, connection, love, and magic were always an arm's length away... until I began working with the shadow—or should I say, the shadow began working on me.

These chapters were never meant to be devoured in a single sitting. Each chapter is an invitation: to look again, to feel deeper, to become intimate with the things that leave us a little unsettled. Not everyone can do this work. But you have. You are. I am here with you. Every day I show up and continue working on my fears, perceived limitations, old stories, and limiting beliefs.

Shadow work is not glamorous, and it doesn't end. It is messy, and beautifully, terribly human. It requires patience and the courage to face the darknesses that others avoid and deny. To feel what others numb.

And yet, here you are, still with me.

This letter is for you... for the part of you who has been poisoned, numbed, decomposed, deceived, and still chooses to return. You are not broken. You are unfolding.

If you've made it here, you've likely encountered resistance. Maybe you closed the book or stepped away from the screen. And maybe you came back. That's what matters. The coming back. The returning to yourself. Returning with a form of intuition that no one can take away. This is true wisdom.

My return did not occur in one singular moment. It was with each perceived failure that I got back up. With each season caught in the underworld, I leaned in and let the wisdom of shadow teach me. Unwinding old programming is a trip, and it rarely feels the way we imagine it will. This is why I think of healing and expansion as a cyclical experience.

Shadow work is spiral work. It is not linear, nor is it final. There will be times you revisit old wounds and think, Haven't I healed this already? But you are not the same self who first began. You now bring new depth, new instincts, and a new vision. You can see in the dark and descend without drowning. That is the wisdom of the spiral. I cannot tell you how many times I lay on the bathroom floor, face stained with tears, praying for my pain to subside. The answer never seemed to arrive in a loud way; it was the slow work I wanted to rush through that became my medicine.

So I ask you not to rush. Let these themes breathe. Come back to them. Let them take root in the beautiful darkness of your psyche. Revisit the fairy tales;

they will call to you if you listen. Reflect on the symbols when your dreams present them.

One of my favorite places is in upstate New York. I cannot count how many times I visited that reflection pool. This pool is a man-made structure, a concrete oval filled with rainwater. There is no movement, and as you look into the water, it appears pitch black... and slowly your reflection appears. This pool was once surrounded by hemlock. These beautiful and poisonous trees created a canopy around the pool. The pool sat in the center, as if cradled by these looming giants.

Although we are not sitting there together, I believe in the power of intention and imagination. So when you need a place to return to, I invite you to conjure up the image of the reflection pool.

Close your eyes, if you can, and imagine this with me. A quiet space. Earth beneath you. Early evening, no one is around. A pool of still water sits before you, unmoving and untouched. You are alone here, but not lonely. This is your place of reflection and contemplation. A place of remembering.

This is an invitation to look inward, allowing the water to mirror the things that are stirring and rising from within. You do not try—just simply see. Patience, stillness, and silence.

The pool asks nothing of you, but will give you an undistorted reflection if you are willing to look closer. It reflects truth—sometimes painful, sometimes radiant. Often, it is both.

You can return to this image as you sit with the material in this book, whenever you feel lost or the world is too full of noise. Let it hold and contain you.

Do not fear what arises in the reflection. Everything that emerges is part of the whole. Even the grotesque and the terrifying... especially the terrifying. It is often the face of fear that conceals our true power.

You are not here to be good or to be liked. You are here to express your crazy, weird, wild ways. That includes the rage, the silence, the grief, the hunger, the madness. Let it all be sacred, because it already is.

We do not transform in spite of the darkness, but because of it. You are transmuting lead into gold and poison into medicine. Your afflictions are not pathologies; they are holy expressions of the psyche.

Thank you for daring to enter the underworld with me.

Your sister in shadow,

Melissa Kim Corter